THE LITTLE BOOK OF WATERFORD

TOM HUNT

First published 2017

The History Press Ireland
50 City Quay
Dublin 2
Ireland
www.thehistorypress.ie

The History Press Ireland is a member of Publishing Ireland,
the Irish book publishers' association.

© Tom Hunt, 2017

The right of Tom Hunt to be identified as the Author
of this work has been asserted in accordance with the
Copyrights, Designs and Patents Act 1988.

All rights reserved. No part of this book may be reprinted
or reproduced or utilised in any form or by any electronic,
mechanical or other means, now known or hereafter invented,
including photocopying and recording, or in any information
storage or retrieval system, without the permission in writing
from the Publishers.

British Library Cataloguing in Publication Data.
A catalogue record for this book is available from the British Library.

ISBN 978 1 84588 906 7

Typesetting and origination by The History Press
Printed and bound by TJ International Ltd.

CONTENTS

	Introduction	5
1.	Waterford Timeline	7
2.	Waterford: Ireland's Oldest City	24
3.	Small Town Waterford	36
4.	Royal Visits	54
5.	Waterford's Built Heritage	63
6.	Waterford Notables	77
7.	Waterford: The City of Crystal	92
8.	Waterford's Decade of Revolution, 1914–24	102
9.	Entertainment	116
10.	Sporting Waterford	130
	Bibliography	142

INTRODUCTION

In the early 1840s, Mr and Mrs S.C. Hall in their *Ireland: Its Scenery, Character and History* wrote that 'Waterford is, perhaps, the least interesting, and certainly the least picturesque of the counties of Ireland; it is, for the most part, barren of trees, and, the soil, naturally poor, has had little advantage from cultivation'. Blinded by their sense of self-importance, Samuel Carter Hall (who was born in Geneva Barracks in Passage East) and his wife Anna Maria could hardly have been more mistaken, although they did accept that 'the approach to Lismore is picturesque and beautiful'. The Comeragh Mountains dominate the county and form a landscape of outstanding natural beauty and stretches of unspoilt wilderness. The Knockmealdown Mountains add to the splendour of west Waterford. The Comeragh's magnificent glacially created corries at Coumshingaun, Crotty's Lake and the Mahon Falls are some of the finest in Ireland as are those at Coumfea and Coumalocha in the Nire Valley. Waterford's long coastline includes a number of sheltered bays and coves with outstanding beaches especially at Ardmore, Bunmahon, Clonea Strand, Dungarvan, Dunmore, Tramore, Stradbally, and Woodstown. Sand spits, sand bars, spectacular cliffs, caves, sea arches, coves and stacks decorate the coastline with the Copper Coast between Tramore and Stradbally granted Geopark status by UNESCO in recognition of the area's special geology.

Waterford is also a county of sophisticated urbanisation with all phases of Ireland's urban history represented. Ardmore and Lismore began as monastic settlements, Waterford is Ireland's oldest city and originated as a Viking settlement; the history of Portlaw is perhaps the most extraordinary of all. Purpose built, on a green-field site, to house the workers of a newly constructed cotton factory, the town's history is truly a tale of wonder.

Waterford is a county of festivals and fairs and sporting excellence and has a history and cultural heritage that is more varied than most counties. This heritage is represented in a variety of forms throughout the county. Time spent on The Mall in Waterford city visiting the museums of Reginald's Tower, the Medieval Museum, the Bishop's Palace, as well as Christ Church Cathedral and the House of Crystal will provide an excellent introduction to this history. Inspiration for this book originated in time spent in the various attractions on The Mall.

This book makes no claim to be a comprehensive history of the city or county. The choice of topics is largely governed by my own personal interests as a social and cultural historian. In truth, a lot of the detail in the book falls into the category of 'stuff I didn't know about the city and county'. Some important aspects (e.g. Waterford as a port city) of the county's history have been largely excluded due to space constraints.

Waterford has been richly endowed with historians whose primary work has been invaluable in writing this *Little Book of Waterford*. These modern-day historians such as Julian Walton, Eamonn McEneaney, John M. Hearne, Willie Fraher, Pat McCarthy, Eugene Broderick, Jack Burtchaell, Des Cowman, Niall Byrne and numerous others are continuing a rich tradition established as early as 1746 by Charles Smith. I am indebted to the staff of the Local Studies sections of the Central Library, Lady Lane, Waterford, the Dungarvan Library, Davitt's Quay, Dungarvan and the Mullingar Branch Library of the Westmeath County Library for facilitating research. Beth Amphlett's editorial input was significant and as always special thanks is due to my wife Mary for her patience and tolerance that facilitates this obsession with historical research.

1

WATERFORD TIMELINE

c. **430**: St Declan introduced Christianity to Waterford and particularly to Ardmore, where he established a monastery and converted the Déisí. According to the twelfth-century *Life of St Declan of Ardmore*, Declan pre-dated Patrick and was made a bishop in Rome. He met Patrick, not yet a bishop, on an Italian road as he made his way home.

c. **637**: St Carthage was expelled from his monastery at Rahan, County Offaly and arrived on the banks of the River Blackwater, where he was gifted land by the king of the Déisí at Lismore. He died shortly afterwards, on 14 May 637. The monastery he founded at Lismore became a famous abbey and proved to be the origin of the town of Lismore.

833: The Vikings travelled up the River Blackwater and plundered and burned Lismore for the first time. By 1113 it had been attacked seven more times.

853: In the mid-ninth century the Vikings began to winter in Ireland and established temporary settlements known as longphorts. One was established in Waterford in 853 that allowed the Vikings to conduct their raids travelling inland via the Suir, Nore and Barrow rivers. This settlement was abandoned by 900.

914: One of the great Viking adventurers, Ragnall, a grandson of Ivan the Boneless, established a new base in Waterford and began an era of permanent Viking settlement in Ireland. This foundation date makes Waterford the oldest city in Ireland.

1096: Malchus, an Irish monk based at the Benedictine monastery of Winchester, was consecrated the first bishop of Viking Waterford by Anselm, the Archbishop of Canterbury.

1170: The English, recruited by Dermot Mac Murrough and commanded by Richard de Clare (more popularly known as Strongbow), landed at Passage, County Waterford and moved inland. With the support of Richard le Gros they captured and destroyed Viking Waterford. After the capture of the city one of the most famous marriages in Irish history was held in Christ Church Cathedral when Strongbow married Dermot Mac Murrough's daughter, Aoife.

1171: Henry II, the first English king to set foot in Ireland, landed at Crooke, close to Passage East, in October and moved inland to Waterford where he received the submission of several Irish chieftains. Henry retained the city of Waterford as his personal possession.

1204: King John granted the citizens of Waterford city the right to hold an annual fair during the last week of August.

1207: In November King John issued a murage grant to the citizens of Waterford that allowed them to retain customs duties levied in the city and invest the revenue in repairing and building city walls.

1215: The first of more than thirty royal charters was granted to Waterford city. Its most important clause granted the citizens of the city the right to hold their property directly from the king and not from any feudal lord. Citizens were entitled to manage their own affairs, to hold their own courts, and to be free of all taxes on goods bought and sold at fairs or transported by land or water anywhere in King John's territory.

1349: Waterford city was ravaged by the Black Death, which wiped out an estimated one-third of the population.

1363: The Diocese of Waterford and Lismore was established with Thomas le Reve as the first bishop of the united diocese.

***c.* 1373:** The economic rivalry between New Ross and Waterford indirectly led to the compilation of the Great Charter Roll, one of the great treasures of medieval Ireland and now on display at the Waterford Medieval Museum. The vellum roll is composed of fifteen separate royal charters and seventeen illustrations. The walled city of Waterford features in the first image and forms the oldest image of an Irish city in existence. The image of the four mayors of the royal cities of Dublin, Waterford, Cork and Limerick are the earliest images of medieval mayors in either Britain or Ireland and those of King Edward III are the only ones in existence created while he was alive. In May 2011 the Great Charter Roll was taken from Waterford to Dublin to enable Queen Elizabeth II to inspect the document on the occasion of her visit to Ireland.

1461: Battles between the citizens of Waterford with the Powers, the most powerful family in rural county Waterford, and their allies the O'Driscolls from Baltimore in Cork were not unusual in medieval Waterford. In 1461 the O'Driscolls landed at Tramore, where they were routed by the mayor and citizens of Waterford.

1495: Perkin Warbeck, a pretender to the English throne, and his forces began an eleven-day siege of Waterford city in July. They were eventually repelled by the citizens of the city, led by the mayor, Robert Butler. The siege earned Waterford the distinction of being the first Irish city to experience an artillery attack. It survived to tell the tale chiefly because of strategically placed cannons on Reginald's Tower. Two of Warbeck's ships were sunk and many aboard were drowned in the Suir. Prisoners were beheaded in the Market Square and the ritual display of heads took place.

1497: Warbeck returned for another attack on the city but was chased out to sea by a small Waterford naval fleet. It is believed that Henry VII showed his appreciation of Waterford's loyalty by awarding the city its motto of *Urbs Intacta manet Waterfordia* (The city of Waterford remains untaken).

1518: Disputes between the ports of Waterford and New Ross for control of the lucrative wine trade, which at times had degenerated into open warfare, finally ended when a force of Waterford merchants accompanied by foreign mercenaries attacked New Ross, sacked the town and confiscated its civic mace. This mace is still in Waterford, displayed in the city's Medieval Museum.

1602: Richard Boyle, later the Great Earl of Cork, purchased the 12,000-acre estate of Sir Walter Raleigh in Cork and Waterford.

Boyle arrived in Ireland virtually penniless and died one of the wealthiest men in the United Kingdom. Boyle rebuilt the towns of Lismore and Tallow, developed iron mines, exported timber and refurbished Lismore Cathedral and Castle. He was also one of the driving forces of the Munster Plantation and introduced English Protestant settlers to his estates.

1618: King James I insisted that all urban mayors take the Oath of Supremacy, which recognised the king as head of the Church. Waterford mayors were reluctant to accept this and Waterford Corporation was abolished. For the first time the city was ruled directly from Dublin.

1626: Waterford had its charter restored by King Charles I. A sum of £3,000 changed hands for this privilege and the Great Charter of Charles I provided the principles by which the city was governed until 1848.

1645: The 1641 rebellion virtually destroyed Lismore. The town also saw battles in 1641, 1643 and 1645 when a force of Catholic confederacy, commanded by Lord Castlehaven, destroyed the castle. The town became a neglected village consisting of a few miserable cabins.

1649: Oliver Cromwell and his New Model Army began an unsuccessful eight-day siege of Waterford city in November. Bad weather, troops' illnesses and the need to find secure winter quarters forced Cromwell to abandon the siege and earned Waterford the distinction of being the only city that Cromwell besieged and failed to capture.

1650: Although Oliver Cromwell failed to secure the surrender of Waterford, the city remained partly under siege and in August 1650 Cromwell's son-in-law, General Ireton, received the surrender of General Thomas, commander of the city garrison.

1655: Members of the Society of Friends (Quakers) first settled in Waterford, near the parish of St John's, in the mid-1650s. By the early nineteenth-century many Waterford Quaker families were prosperous landowners, millers, farmers, merchants, industrialists, ship-owners and shipbuilders. They formed a powerful business community in Waterford city which extended along the Suir valley as far as Clonmel. Members of the Beale, Gatchell, Grubb, Jacob, Malcomson, Penrorse,

Pim, Strangman and White families exercised an influence in industry and commerce disproportionate to their numerical presence.

1690: Coffee house culture was introduced to Ireland in the 1690s and began in Waterford city where it is believed that Ireland's first coffee house was established in 1690. Green coffee was traded at the port, then roasted, brewed and sold at John Akenhead's Coffee House on what became Coffee House Lane in Waterford.

1717: The Beresford dynasty was introduced to Waterford when Sir Marcus Beresford married Lady Catherine Power, heir to the Power estate centred at Curraghmore. Beresford was the wealthy owner of a considerable estate at Coleraine, County Derry. Catherine Power was the only female heir to the vast Curraghmore property in the family's long history and was just four months short of her fifteenth birthday when the marriage took place.

1737: The urban streetscape of Waterford was dramatically changed when a new wide street, The Mall, was laid out.

1742: Highwayman William Crotty was hanged in Waterford on 18 March. Crotty planned his raids from his hideout in the Comeragh Mountains until he was betrayed by an accomplice, David Norris. He was captured in February 1742 and following his hanging his head was placed on a spike at the county jail at Ballybricken.

1748: The Cavendish line was introduced to Lismore when, on 27 March, Charlotte Boyle married William Cavendish, the future 4th Duke of Devonshire and Prime Minister of Great Britain. Lismore Castle and the lands of the Boyle estate passed to the Devonshire family. Today Lismore Castle is the Irish base of the 12th Duke of Devonshire.

1774: The Bishop of Waterford Dr Richard Chenevix and the members of the corporation decided to demolish the city's Christ Church Cathedral, with its unfashionable Gothic architecture. The destruction, at a cost of £150, led to the discovery of a magnificent set of fifteenth-century Benedictine copes and High Mass vestments which are now on display at the Medieval Museum. The vestments, hidden in the cathedral vaults in 1650, to protect them from Cromwell's army, provide a rare example of Renaissance art in Ireland and are the only set of pre-Reformation High Mass

vestments to survive in Ireland and the only full set of medieval vestments surviving in northern Europe.

1783: The uncle-and-nephew partnership of George and William Penrose established a glass-manufacturing business in Waterford. The Penroses were one of the first Quaker families to make a significant impact on the economy of Waterford. In October 1783, an advertisement in the *Dublin Evening Post* stated that they could 'supply all kinds of plain or cut flint glass' for 'ready money'.

c. **1785:** Thomas Dunn took possession of a River Mahon-powered oat mill at Kilmacthomas. This began a Flahavan association with the mill that continues to the present day. Dunn was the great-great-great-grandfather of John Flahavan who is the current managing director of the iconic Flahavan Company. In 1935 it was decided to expand the mill and an oat-flaking facility was installed. In 1959 the construction of the current Flahavan six-storey mill building was completed. The company manufactures Flahavan's Progress Oatlets, Ireland's leading porridge oats product, as well as a variety of other healthy cereal products and exports to Britain, the US, South Korea, Russia, India, and Spain.

1789: Dr Francis Barker acquired a house on John's Hill in Waterford city and converted it to the Waterford Fever Hospital; this hospital is regarded as the first of its kind in Ireland and only the second such institution to be opened in the British Empire.

Waterford Timeline 13

1794: Waterford's links with the outside world were significantly improved when the first bridge across the River Suir, affectionately known as Timbertoes, was built. This privately funded timber toll bridge, supported by forty sets of oak piers, was built by the American builder Lemuel Cox at a cost of £14,000; another £13,000 was paid to the ferrymen to buy out their rights. Timbertoes continued as a toll bridge until 1907.

1798: Education in Waterford city received a significant boost when three Presentation Sisters arrived in Waterford and set up the city's first school for the education of poor Catholic girls. Newtown School for the education of members of the Society of Friends was also established the same year, opening in August.

1806: Charles Bianconi arrived in Waterford and set up a shop in George's Street. He later moved to Clonmel and began his coach-transport company. In 1832 Bianconi purchased the house of Thomas Meagher, located on the Quay, and this became the terminus of the Bianconi transport network in Waterford. Today it trades as the Granville Hotel.

1816: The greatest shipping tragedy off the coast of County Waterford happened on 31 January, when the *Seahorse*, carrying the soldiers and families of the 2nd Battalion, 59th (2nd Nottinghamshire) Regiment, who were returning to Ireland after the Battle of Waterloo, was wrecked in Tramore Bay. Of the 394 people on board only 30 – all men, including the ship's master and two seamen – survived.

1816: Education for the wealthy young girls of Waterford was provided with the arrival of the nuns of the Ursuline Order, who established their first convent in the city at Waterpark.

1816: Gas lighting, using gas manufactured by the firm of B & J Graham, was introduced to Waterford, the first Irish city to benefit from the facility. In October, Timbertoes was illuminated at night.

1825: In April David Malcomson, a sixty-one-year-old industrialist and member of the Society of Friends, leased 19 acres of land at Mayfield, Portlaw, where he built a cotton mill for spinning, weaving and dyeing cloth, and the new industrial town of Portlaw developed. In 1828 Malcomson estimated that £60,000 had been invested on construction and by 1846 an additional £40,000 had been spent.

1826: A major step on the road to Catholic emancipation was achieved with the victory of Henry Villiers-Stuart, a liberal Protestant landlord, over the sitting MP Lord George Thomas Beresford, a member of one of the most powerful political dynasties in the United Kingdom, in the Waterford constituency in the 1826 General Election. The *Dublin Evening Post* explained the significance of the election: 'It will be a battle ... which will decide the Catholic question ... The election of Mr Stuart must be considered as the harbinger of civil freedom in Ireland.'

1832: Trappist monks, expelled from their monastery at Mellary, near Nantes in France, established a monastery at Scrahan, close to Cappoquin in the Knockmealdown Mountains, in an abandoned cottage on 600 acres of marginal land donated rent-free by Sir Richard Keane. The monks' new headquarters was renamed Mount Mellary in memory of their former French base.

1832: An outbreak of cholera, which ravaged the poor of Waterford city, began in July and was responsible for close to 300 deaths before it finally abated.

1835: The first Theatre Royal, located in Bolton Street, Waterford, opened for business in February with a performance of *The Mountaineers*.

1839: The Poor Law Act (1838) made the provision of relief for the poor in Ireland compulsory for the first time. Waterford city and county were divided into three Poor Law unions in March 1839: Dungarvan, Waterford city and Lismore. The Lismore workhouse, with accommodation for 600, opened in April 1841, followed by Dungarvan workhouse in May 1842 and Waterford workhouse in July 1844.

1843: Daniel O'Connell's campaign for repeal was founded on a series of nationwide mass meetings addressed by the great orator who believed that mass mobilisation was the only means of convincing the British Government to grant political independence. The greatest mass meeting held in Waterford was staged in Ballybricken on 8 July 1843 and was attended by an estimated, but surely exaggerated, 300,000 people.

1845: Frederick Douglass, an escaped American slave and anti-slavery crusader, published the *Narrative of Frederick Douglass*

– *An American Slave* in 1845 and arrived in Ireland for a four-month lecture tour. On 9 October, at the City Hall, he addressed the people of Waterford on the evils of slavery.

1845: The first official recorded reference to the Great Famine in the county was made in October when the Dungarvan Resident Magistrate G. Fitzgerald wrote to the under secretary that 'the potatoe [*sic*] crops appears to be universally blighted'. The arrival of the blight in Waterford was first reported in the *Cork Examiner* in September 1845. During the decade of the great famine (1841–51) the population of the city and county declined by 32,136 between 1841 and 1851.

1848: On 7 March, Thomas Francis Meagher, a native of the city and a leader of the Young Irelanders, flew a tricolour from a house at 33 The Mall, Waterford, which had been adopted as the flag of the Wolfe Tone Confederate Club. The flag flew for a week before being removed by the authorities. The tricolour was later adopted as the national flag for Ireland.

1850: Brothers William and Robert Jacob established a biscuit-manufacturing business in Bridge Street, Waterford, in September.

1851: The first attempt at establishing a glass-manufacturing industry ended when the proprietor George Gatchell offered for sale his 'entire stock of glass, including dinner and table lamps, gas chandeliers, one crystal chandelier for six lights, together with beautiful specimens of Bohemian and Venetian Glass'.

1853: The Waterford and Kilkenny railway line reached Dunkitt, just outside the city.

1853: On 5 September the Waterford–Tramore railway line was opened and the company directors and 200 guests were carried from Waterford to Tramore on the maiden voyage. Such was the novelty of the occasion that one of the Waterford newspapers reported that 'all the fields along the route were dotted with people all out to catch a glimpse of the new wonder … the iron horse that pulls the cars behind it … mothers clutched their children and pressed further back from the strange sight'.

1857: The Peoples' Park in Waterford city was formally opened by the lord lieutenant, Lord Carlisle, on 19 August 1857. A bandstand was added in 1869, a fountain in 1883 and a cycling track in 1891.

1861: One of Waterford's iconic landmarks, the clock tower, with its freshwater drinking fountains and four clock faces, was completed. Charles Tarrant was the engineer responsible for the clock's design.

1862: Between 1846 and 1882 forty ships were built at the Malcomson Brothers-owned Neptune Ironworks in Waterford. The launch of the SS *Cella* in September 1862 began the transatlantic liner-building phase of the company and the liner initiated the London–Le Havre–New York route for the line owned by Malcomson Brothers. This phase of Waterford's shipbuilding industry came to an end on 6 May 1867 with the launch of the giant 1,572-ton *Indiana*. At almost 100m in length, it was the largest ship ever built in Waterford and the last ocean liner built in the city.

1864: The last public hanging in Waterford was held on 14 April, following the conviction of Thomas Walsh for the murder of an elderly farmer, Thomas Connolly. The hanging took place outside the gaol at Ballybricken and was witnessed by a crowd of between 2,000 and 3,000 people.

1867: In June, the *Erin's Hope* arrived off the coast of Waterford at Helvick Head, An Rinn from New York with arms, ammunition and forty members of the Fenian Brotherhood. A fishing-boat skipper took thirty-two Fenians ashore, landing them on the beach near Ballinagoul pier. George Jones, a coastguard in Helvic, saw them and alerted the RIC, who set out in pursuit. Most of the men

were arrested but all were eventually freed; the *Erin's Hope* was forced to return to America without landing its military cargo.

1867: The Little Sisters of the Poor arrived in Waterford and took up residence at a house in Adelphi Terrace. Five years later the foundation stone for the first Irish convent of the Little Sisters of the Poor was laid at Manor Hill, Waterford.

1868: The coursing greyhound, Master McGrath, won the first of his three Waterloo Cup victories, the premier coursing event in the United Kingdom. Master McGrath was owned by Lord Lurgan and was born in Colligan Lodge, near Dungarvan, where Lord Lurgan owned a hunting lodge.

1875: Work on building a reservoir at Knockaderry, 10 miles from the city, capable of supplying Waterford city with clean, fresh water began. When completed the artificial lake stretched to over 82 acres.

1876: The extraordinary success story of the Malcomson multi-national, multi-faceted business empire ended in June 1876 in the court of bankruptcy where the firm of Malcomson Brothers presented an account that showed liabilities amounting to £551,894 and combined assets of £202,094.

1877: The honorary Freedom of the City award was introduced and on 6 February Waterford Corporation awarded the first honorary freedom to Isaac Butt, leader of the Home Rule Party. In 1880 Charles Stewart Parnell received the honour.

1879: A native of Lismore, Vere St Leger Goold was defeated by Revd John Hartley in the Wimbledon Lawn Tennis Final – the only occasion that a member of the clergy has won the title. St Leger Goold too made a piece of history: in 1907, he was convicted of murder, the only Wimbledon finalist to achieve such an unwanted distinction.

1895: A Waterford-owned horse, 'The Wild Man from Borneo', owned by horse dealer John Widger and ridden by his brother Joe, won the Grand National. It was reported that every man, woman and child had wagered on the horse and Ballybricken was ablaze with bonfires for a week after the race. Three Widger brothers, Joe, Tom and Mike, rode in the 1896 race.

1895: Dungarvan's greatest sea tragedy occurred on 24 December 1895 when the *Moresby* sank in Dungarvan Harbour. On 21 December, the *Moresby* left Cardiff carrying a cargo of 1,778 tons of coal bound for Chile. After encountering a storm, the ship took refuge and dropped anchor in the harbour three days later. During the night the *Moresby* broke anchor, capsized and twenty of the twenty-five crew and passengers were drowned.

1896: X-ray was used for the first time in Ireland on 13 April 1896 at De La Salle Teacher Training College, Waterford, when Brother Potamian (Michael Francis O'Reilly), Professor of Physics at the college, conducted an examination on a woman with an injured hand.

1897: In 1892 the bacon curers of Waterford and Limerick began buying pigs directly from the farmers and sidelining the pig buyers whose great stronghold in Waterford was in Ballybricken. In 1897 the dispute escalated and the pig buyers resorted to violence. Incidents of assault, intimidation, damage to property and riot were daily occurrences. An estimated 8,000 people attended a rally in Ballybricken in support of the buyers and their belated defenders the pork butchers. Dennys and Mattersons were forced into temporary closure. Richardsons remained open for business but a serious riot took place outside the factory gates on 29 December. In January an additional 155 policemen were drafted into the city, almost one for every pig buyer, and the violence gradually lessened. In July the Pig Buyers' Association accepted a settlement that greatly reduced their influence.

1900: The last hanging in Waterford was carried out behind the walls of Ballybricken Jail on 10 April. Patrick Dunphy, a seventy-four-year-old widower, had been convicted of murdering two of his sons by strychnine poisoning.

1903: The Waterford Corporation became the first in Ireland to declare St Patrick's Day a general holiday throughout the city and to entirely suspend business on that day. Later in the year the Bank Holiday (Ireland) Act made St Patrick's Day a national holiday.

1904: The last royal visit to Waterford took place on 5 May when Edward VII and Queen Alexandra visited the city and later travelled by train to Lismore where they were the guests of the Duke of Devonshire at Lismore Castle. At the railway station, prior to leaving the city, Edward knighted the mayor, James Power. He was the tenth and last Mayor of Waterford to receive a knighthood.

1912: Dr Mary Strangman became the first woman elected to Waterford Corporation. She was also the city's first female doctor. A month later Lily Poole was also elected to the corporation.

1913: A new bridge, named the Redmond Bridge, was opened in February by John Redmond. The bridge replaced the privately owned Timbertoes, which had served the city for over 120 years.

1918: Over 1,100 Waterford people died in the First World War. The last Waterford casualty of the conflict was the unfortunate William Hales, a native of Brown Street, Portlaw who was killed on 10 November 1918, on the eve of the war ending. At the time of his enlistment Hales resided in Detroit, USA, and was serving in the Canadian Infantry.

1929: Postman Laurence Griffin completed his rounds on Christmas Day in Stradbally and was last seen in the vicinity of Whelan's Hotel and public house. Griffin disappeared overnight and the 'Case of the Missing Postman' became a public and media sensation. Three months later ten people, including two policemen, were charged with his murder, mainly based on the evidence of Jim Fitzgerald who withdrew his statement shortly after the trial commenced. Eventually the case was withdrawn by the state prosecutor; Justice Finlay ordered it to be dismissed and concluded by stating that 'nothing in the evidence put before me implicates any one of the defendants with any of the charges'.

1943: Tragedy struck Waterford City during the early morning of 4 March when a section of the perimeter wall of Ballybricken Jail collapsed on to houses in King's Terrace, killing nine and injuring eighteen, one of whom later died. Although the jail had been closed since 1939, turf was stored there, stacked against the prison walls. The walls were unable to withstand the pressure and collapsed.

1947: In April building work began on the site of a new glass factory at Ballytruckle. The industry that was to define Waterford internationally was reintroduced to the city by Charles Bačik, an émigré from Czechoslovakia. Bačik recruited a fellow Czech, Miroslav Havel, as his first employee and Havel became the key design person in the plant until his retirement in 1990.

1947: Newly elected USA Congressman, John Fitzgerald Kennedy paid his first significant visit to Ireland in September 1947 and made Lismore Castle his base for a three-week visit. Hosted by his sister Kathleen, during the stay John Kennedy paid an unannounced visit to his ancestral family and home at Dunganstown, County Wexford, for the first time. He later claimed that this visit was 'filled with magic sentiment' and that he left the house 'in a flow of nostalgia and sentiment'. Later in the year, the Kennedy matriarch Rose and Kathleen's sister Patricia visited Lismore Castle. Rose found 'a picture-book castle, with grey walls covered in moss – green and soft – and ivy on the outer turning red now in the autumn'. 'It is beautiful here beyond words, quiet, peaceful, secluded' she wrote to her husband Joe.

1948: The Waterford senior hurlers, captained by the veteran goalkeeper Jim Ware, won the county's first All-Ireland senior hurling title on 5 September, defeating Dublin 6-7 to 4-2. In what was a great day for Waterford hurling the county's minor team also won the All-Ireland title.

1957: One of the greatest shocks in the history of Gaelic football happened in June 1957 when Waterford defeated Kerry in the first round of the Munster senior football championship by a single point (2-5 to 0-10).

1959: Waterford, captained by Frankie Walsh, won its second and to-date last All-Ireland senior hurling title, this time defeating Kilkenny (3-12 to 1-10) after drawing the initial match 1-17 to 5-5.

1962: On 2 April Waterford's Royal Showband topped the bill at the Empire Theatre, Liverpool. Their support act was a comparatively unknown local band called The Beatles. A month later the Royal Showband had the distinction of becoming the first showband to enter the Irish charts when their first record, 'Come Down the Mountain Katie Daly', featuring Tom Dunphy, reached number 8.

1966: A new era for industry in Waterford began in November when the mayor, Alderman Patrick Browne, turned the sod on the industrial estate in the city. The first factory on the estate, the pharmaceutical company Hadensa, opened in July 1967. In 1980, 2,300 people were employed at the estate.

1968: In September Waterford FC were beaten 3-1 by the reigning European Champions, Manchester United, in the opening round of the European Cup. The match was played at Lansdowne Road in Dublin before a crowd of 45,000 who paid 4*s* for entry to the terraces and 10*s* or 12*s* for entry to the stands. It was the first soccer match played at Lansdowne Road. The first of many.

1970: Third-level education returned to Waterford in September 1970 when the Waterford Regional Technical College formally opened its doors to students.

1973: An attempt to land a consignment of arms from Libya destined for the IRA was foiled when the *Claudia* was intercepted by the Irish navy close to Helvick Head, An Rinn. Those arrested included veteran republican Joe Cahill, OC of the Belfast Brigade of the IRA, who told the Special Criminal Court that his only crime was not 'getting the contents of the *Claudia* into the hands of the freedom fighters in this country'.

1980: Brian Gardner's goal gave Waterford FC a 1–0 victory against St Patrick's Athletic in the FAI Cup final; this was only the club's second victory in the main knockout competition in Irish domestic soccer.

1982: Work began on the construction of a new bridge across the River Suir at Waterford after the Redmond Bridge was deemed unsafe; the first two lanes of the bridge were officially opened in 1984 with work completed in 1986. The 204m bridge was named the Brother Edmund Ignatius Rice Bridge.

1984: John Treacy, from Villierstown, County Waterford, racing in his first marathon, won the silver medal in the Los Angeles Olympic Games, finishing second behind Carlos Lopes in a time of 2:09:56.

1985: Waterford Regional Airport opened for business. On 5 July, the first international scheduled flight, a Ryanair flight to Gatwick Airport, took off from the newly built airport; it was also the first scheduled flight from a non-state airport in Ireland.

1986: The mare Dawn Run, owned by Waterford's Charmain Hill, made racing history when she won the Gold Cup at Cheltenham.

Dawn Run remains the only horse to win the Gold Cup and Champion Hurdle double at Cheltenham.

1989: On 8 September, Waterford local radio WLR FM began broadcasting after it received the franchise for public broadcasting in the Waterford region.

1993: The two-day Fleadh Mór in Tramore on 3-4 July 1993 almost certainly presented the greatest collection of musical royalty to perform at a festival in Ireland. The Fleadh Mór was promoted by Kilmacthomas-native Vince Power and his Mean Fiddler organisation and featured Bob Dylan, Ray Charles, Jerry Lee Lewis, Van Morrison, The Chieftains, Moving Hearts, John Prine, Nancy Griffith, A Woman's Heart, Christy Moore, Joan Baez, Shane MacGowan, The Pogues, Sharon Shannon and several others.

2009: On 5 January, news of the receievership of Waterford Wedgwood Ltd was released, and on 30 January it was announced that the Waterford Crystal plant in Kilbarry was to close immediately, with a loss of 480 jobs.

2009: The largest infrastructural project in the county's history was completed when, on 19 October, the Minister for Arts, Sports and Tourism, Martin Cullen TD, officially opened the Waterford bypass road network, which included 22.6km of dual carriageway. The project provided a second crossing of the River Suir 3.5km downstream from the Rice Bridge. The 465m-long cable-stay bridge, constructed between May 2006 and October 2009, carried the dual carriageway across the River Suir between Waterford and Kilkenny. The bridge, completed at a cost of €55 million, with a main span of 230m, the longest in the Republic of Ireland, is supported by a single reinforced concrete pylon that reaches 117m above foundation level. The pylon supports the main span with a modified-fan cable arrangement using seventy-six cables that measure 11,900m. Over 6,700 cubic metres of concrete were used in the bridge construction. The project included sixty principal structures including five viaducts, ten overbridges, five road underbridges, three railway underbridges, three river underbridges and eight accommodation underpasses. The project was one of the first public-private partnership (PPP) road projects to be completed in Ireland.

2010: The Michelin Guide awarded The House Restaurant at the Cliff House Hotel in Ardmore a prestigious star, the first time a hotel restaurant in Ireland achieved the distinction. The Michelin Star has been retained each year since.

2012: In June the Dawn Meats beef processing plant at Carroll's Cross, near Kilmacthomas began manufacturing beef burgers exclusively for fast-food giant McDonald's after a €300 million contract was signed between the multi-nationals. The plant produces more than 400 million beef burgers annually with product destined for markets in Ireland, the UK and Continental Europe, processing approximately 40,000 tonnes of Irish beef annually. In June 2016, a significant milestone was reached when Dawn Meats announced that it had produced its one billionth beef burger for McDonald's.

2013: The Waterford blaa, a soft, floury white bread roll that traces its origins back to the arrival of the French Huguenots in the city in the 1690s, was awarded Protected Geographic Indication (PGI) status by the European Commission. The scheme recognises products whose links to a region make them unique. The blaa is made with a simple white flour, yeast, water and salt dough, and the rolls are traditionally dusted with flour before baking. There are four members of the Waterford Blaa Bakers Association – M&D Bakery, Hickey's Bakery, Kilmacow Bakery and Barron's Bakery.

2015: Louise Richardson, a Tramore native who was educated at the Ursuline Convent, Waterford, was the first of her family to attend university. A graduate of Trinity College and Harvard, she became one of the leading experts on international terrorism. In 2009, she was appointed Principal of the University of St Andrews, the first woman and the first Roman Catholic since the Reformation to occupy the position. In June 2015, she was appointed Vice-Chancellor of Oxford University, the first woman to hold the post since it was initiated in 1230.

2016: Work on the Waterford Greenway, built on a 45km section of the disused railway line from Dungarvan to Waterford, was completed and opened as a walkway and cycling track.

2

WATERFORD: IRELAND'S OLDEST CITY

THE VIKING SETTLEMENT AT WOODSTOWN

One of the finest archaeological discoveries in recent years was made in County Waterford at Woodstown, on the southern bank of the River Suir approximately 9km upstream from Reginald's Tower. The site was declared a national monument in May 2005 when its full significance was realised. D-shaped riverside Viking sites with the riverbank forming the straight side of the D are common across Europe but the Woodstown double-D site was of a different order. Archaeologists believe that a D-shaped enclosure was initially developed at Woodstown and at a later stage the ramparts were extended to form a double-D or what might be more accurately described as a B-shaped enclosure of 29,100 square metres. Information unearthed during the archaeological dig provided remarkable new insights into the Viking history of Waterford.

The dig unearthed 6,007 artefacts. Most were of iron but some stone objects, including whetstones and rotary grindstones used to sharpen tools and weapons, ceramic material and a small amount of organic material were also found. The discovery of a Viking burial ground with male grave goods was one of the most significant discoveries at the site. These included a sword, a spearhead, a shield boss, a knife, bone, a ringed pin, a whetstone and two copper-alloy mounts, which almost certainly belonged to a Viking warrior or other high-status individual. The landward sides of the settlement were surrounded by defensive ramparts, which consisted of a ditch and bank topped with oblique-angled palisade fencing.

Waterford: Ireland's Oldest City 25

Woodstown was a centre of commercial activity between *c*. 850 and *c*. 950. In the words of archaeologist Maurice F. Hurley, 'The site was both a hive of industry and a commercial centre to which the talents and traditions of many lands were drawn.' Evidence of industry, especially metalwork, was clear. The volume of waste, particularly of iron slag, implied that the scale of industrial activity at Woodstown was of greater significance than one just catering for the settlement itself. The discovery of an iron-smelting furnace was significant as this technique was not in general use in Ireland at the time but was in widespread use in northwest Europe, especially in areas with a Viking presence. In contrast, smithing carried out in Woodstown was in the Irish tradition and indicative of the importance of the maintenance of sharp edges on tools and weapons to the inhabitants. Commercial activities were suggested by the discovery of lead weights, hack-silver, silver ingots and cut-up items such as Arabic coins and objects of precious metals; the latter included both secular and ecclesiastical native-Irish objects. Only one semi-complete house ground plan was unearthed.

There may be scope for debate on whether the Woodstown stronghold amounted to a typical Viking-type *longphort*, but the archaeological evidence is indisputable that 'this is the first archaeologically proven ninth-century Viking riverside settlement in Ireland'. The iron nails, roves and rivets discovered in Woodstown are clearly associated with the Scandinavian boat-building tradition and while large seagoing vessels may not have been built in Woodstown, boat repairing certainly took place. A number of

roves found at Woodstown were cut and this is indicative of the break-up and repair of boats; the nails are evidence of the presence of Scandinavian-type boats.

There is no specific mention of the Woodstown settlement in the historical (written) record and the archaeological record is silent on the reasons for the abandonment of the site, but it is suggested that its success may have led to its ultimate failure and its industry may have outgrown its infrastructure. The settlement's metalworking industry necessitated the loading and unloading of bulky cargo and this took place at a point where the currents of the River Suir were particularly fast and unsuitable for the construction of jetties close to the settlement. Woodstown may have been abandoned in favour of a more suitable port site at Waterford city.

WATERFORD: THE VIKING CITY FOUNDED BY RAGNALL

Waterford is the only Irish city to retain its Old Norse-derived place name: Waterford is a corruption of the Viking *Vedrar-fjordr*. *Port Láirge*, which is used by the early annalists, is believed to commemorate Láirge, an early Viking leader. In the mid-ninth century, the Vikings began to winter in Ireland and established their earliest permanent settlements, *longphorts*. A temporary *longphort* was established in Waterford in the mid-850s and this provided a strategically placed base that allowed the Vikings to launch raids inland, travelling via the Suir, Nore and Barrow rivers. In 914 one of their great adventurers, Ragnall, established a new base in Waterford and began an era of permanent Viking settlement in Ireland. According to the annals, Ragnall's fleet originated in northern France and landed in Waterford after failing to establish a base in the Severn estuary. The annals recorded that 'a great fleet of Norwegians landed at Port Láirge and they plundered Northern Ossary and brought great spoils and many cows and livestock to their ships'. In 918, Ragnall expanded his base and conducted a successful raid on the Danish Viking city of York; he died in 921 as King of Waterford and York.

Viking Waterford was a triangular structure built on a tidal inlet at the confluence of the St John's River and the Suir. Foreign vessels trading with Waterford docked at the Suir Quay; only Viking ships had access to the St John River. Viking Waterford was protected by a fort known as Dundory Fort, located close to the site of the present-day Reginald's Tower. Archaeological evidence suggests that a wide ditch enclosed this fort. A 3m-high bank, 10-11m wide with a wooden walkway and breastwork on top, and a ditch 2m deep enclosed the ground between the two rivers. The triangular-shaped settlement was traversed by three main streets, which ran from east to west and parallel to the river. The most important of these was High Street, which dominated the commercial life of the city, running parallel to it was Peter Street and, further back from the river, Lady Lane. Four shorter streets running from north to south crossed these three streets and all combined to form a regular street pattern. In its Viking phase Waterford city was destroyed at least four times: in 1031, 1037, 1088 and 1111. In 1137 Diarmait Mac Murchada, King of Leinster, unsuccessfully attacked the city, leaving much destruction.

Archaeological evidence from digs conducted in the 1980s and 1990s has provided a remarkable insight into the nature of Viking Waterford. Seventy-two sub-rectangular houses, with straight sides and round corners, dating to the eleventh and twelfth century, were unearthed; the majority were single-roomed dwellings with thatched roofs and wattle and daub double-woven walls. A hearth was located in the middle of each floor with the smoke escaping through the door or a hole in the roof.

Oats were the most common grain used for food in Viking Waterford and provided the raw material for porridge, bread and ale. Cattle bones were the most common bones discovered and most of the remainder was pig bone. Sheep and goats were rare with red deer antler forming the raw material for tools and jewellery.

Over time the initially pagan Vikings adopted Christianity and the religious practices of the native Irish. The Vikings worshipped in Christ Church Cathedral, built on the site of the current cathedral, in addition to St Olaf's and St Peter's. In 1096 Malchus was consecrated the first Bishop of Waterford.

THE ANGLO-NORMAN MEDIEVAL CITY

Waterford became an Anglo-Norman settlement after the arrival of the English in 1170. A major wall-building programme started in Waterford within a few decades of the English colonisation. The original defences were strengthened during the reign of King John and at least three new stone gates, Coldenbeck Gate, St Martin's Gate and Arundell Gate, were constructed prior to 1212. Reginald's Tower was rebuilt and the Norman development to the west of the original city, including Barronstrand Street and John's Street and a range of irregular narrow streets and lanes that were typical of the medieval period, was enclosed.

The work was funded by a murage grant. These grants were of fixed-term duration and specified what tolls could be charged on incoming goods to fund the wall-building programme. Between 1224 and 1246 three murage grants were granted to fund the building of the walls. The 1243 grant levied a tax of one penny on every 100 salmon, conger and mullet that came through the city gates. A halfpenny was paid on every 100 skins of lambs, kid and squirrel and two pence on every 100 pounds of wax or pepper. The earthen embankments with a palisade fence on top and ditches at the front were replaced by stone walls, gateways and towers so that by the end of the Middle Ages the entire circuit formed a single enclosure. By the mid-1400s the city was defended by fifteen gates and twenty-three mural towers. St John's Gate to the south and St Patrick's Gate to the west provided the main points of entry to the city.

The thirteenth century was a time of general prosperity. Waterford experienced an influx of migrants with merchant families settling in the city from England, Wales, Flanders, Italy and western France. Waterford's sphere of influence expanded significantly as a result as each market brought knowledge of and contact with new places. By the end of the thirteenth century Waterford was a city of significant wealth. At least ten churches were located within the city walls and new religious orders, including the Franciscans, Dominicans and Benedictines, arrived in the city. The latter order was endowed by King John, as was Christ Church Cathedral; his successor, Henry III, gave permission for Waterford's citizens to provide land to the Dominican Order who began building a friary at Blackfriars in 1226. The Dominicans opened schools, educating the sons of the wealthy merchant classes of Waterford. The Franciscan church, known as the French Church, was built around 1240 and, according to tradition, was financed by Sir Hugh Purcell, an Anglo-Norman knight. The Franciscans ministered to the poor and they too received an endowment from Henry III in the form of an annual allowance for the purchase of new habits, which were made from the cheapest available grey cloth. They consequently became known as greyfriars and the street in which the ruins stand is today known as Greyfriars Street. Both monasteries were dissolved on the orders of Henry VIII in 1540 and the Dominican premises was subsequently used as an alms-house (until 1815); its choir was used as a house of worship by the French Huguenots, who were encouraged to settle in the city after the 1690s.

The immediate impact of the Reformation in Waterford was proprietorial rather than devotional; Henry Walsh, a prosperous merchant received a charter from Henry VIII to convert the Franciscan friary to an almshouse. Another member of a Catholic family, William Wyse, was granted the dissolved Benedictine monastery and its lands and the family moved to the Manor of St John.

Waterford's thirteenth-century prosperity did not survive. The Black Death (1349), a switch in the focus of the wine trade from France to Spain and Portugal, the city's rivalry with New Ross and the attacks of the Dunhill-based Power family and their allies, the O'Driscolls from Baltimore in Cork, all had a negative impact on the city. During the reign of Henry VIII Waterford's defences received their first upgrade since the thirteenth century. Waterford's mural towers underwent some modification consequent to the developments of small guns and cannon; Reginald's Tower and the French Tower had two floors added. Arrow loops in the towers and curtain walls were enlarged to form gun ports. Between 1560 and 1568, a new blockhouse tower was built out into the River Suir in front of Reginald's Tower with seven or eight large bronze cannon in anticipation of a Spanish attack that failed to materialise.

The reign of Elizabeth I was an era of much change and although a city of strong Catholicism, Waterford remained loyal to the Crown. The city acted as a military base for royal troops during the Nine Years' War (1594–1603). James I (1603–1625) was not as certain of the city's loyalty and during his reign a star-shaped fort was built outside St Patrick's Gate. This fort was capable of supporting heavy artillery and commanded the city and the river from its height. In 1617, James took away the city's charters but they were restored by his successor, Charles I.

DECONSTRUCTING THE MEDIEVAL CITY

Waterford cast off its medieval clothing in the eighteenth century and transformed into an elegant European city. In the 1690s, demolition of the internal wall of the city began. Demolition of the gates began in 1695. Long stretches of the Quay wall were also removed in the 1700s, opening the Quay frontage to the River Suir. In 1711, the blockhouse in front of Reginald's Tower was taken down. Six of the original towers survived as did sections of the city walls and today Waterford has one of the finest medieval defences of any Irish city, most notably the cylindrical Watch Tower, the Double Tower and the kidney-shaped French Tower.

A series of legislative measures known as the Penal Laws were enacted between 1695 and 1710, excluding Catholics and Nonconformists from public and commercial life. Although many wealthy Waterford Catholic families emigrated, those who remained were relatively unaffected by the legislative restrictions. As early as 1704, Waterford Corporation dropped commercial restrictions against Catholics and others as a result of 'the great decay of trade in the city'. Although excluded from civic office, they were allowed to become freemen from 1710 onwards. Waterford had Presbyterian, Baptist and Quaker meeting houses and three Catholic mass houses by 1740.

CREATING THE MALL

The city was transformed between 1700 and 1750, a process that reflected the wealth and confidence of the ruling classes and the cross-cultural cooperation in the city. The most dramatic change was the creation of The Mall in the 1730s. The St John's River was diverted and the area it occupied and surrounding marshland reclaimed. Charles Smith, writing in 1746, provides a near-contemporary description of the newly created area:

> The Mall is a beautiful walk, about 200 yards long and proportionably broad ... it is planted with rows of Elms, and the sides of the walks are fenced with a stone wall ... Here the Ladies and Gentlemen assemble on fine evenings where they

have the opportunity of each other's conversation. Nothing can be more agreeable than to see this shady walk crowded with the fair sex of the city, taking the air, enjoying the charms of a pleasant evening, and improving their healths …

A bowling green was also laid out on The Mall, introducing a culture of genteel recreation to the city. Smith described it as 'a pleasant Bowling-green for the diversion of the citizens, which is a most innocent and healthful exercise, where in summer time after the business of the day is ended, they sometimes recreate themselves'.

After the demolition of the city's medieval defenses, the wealthy merchants began to build three- and four-storey homes along the Quay overlooking the Suir. This introduced a new architectural style to the city: the houses, with their gables to the front, were known as Dutch Billies. The building of the Exchange, the meeting place of the corporation and the merchants, was completed in 1714.

THE BISHOP'S PALACE

The area running parallel to The Mall was also transformed. Charles Este, the Church of Ireland Bishop of Waterford and Lismore, commissioned Richard Castle to design the Bishop's Palace. This became the finest eighteenth-century ecclesiastical palace in Ireland. Castle's architectural portfolio included Leinster House in Dublin's Kildare Street, the Rotunda Hospital, Carton House in Kildare and Westport House in Mayo. In the manner of Leinster House, the palace is Classical in style and has two principal facades; one facing The Mall and the other the cathedral. The visual impact of the finely cut ashlar limestone was enhanced by the grouping of windows, its pediments and the inclusion of other Classical details such as niches. Part of the medieval town wall was demolished to create a terraced garden. The building was unfinished at the time of Bishop Este's death in 1745 and his successor, Bishop Chenevix, recruited Waterford architect John Roberts to complete the work. This was his first major work in the city and led to further commissions in Waterford.

JOHN ROBERTS' IMPACT

John Roberts (1712–1726), in the words of Eamonn McEneaney, was the man who transformed medieval Waterford into an eighteenth-century European city. Roberts received most of his formal training in carpentry and architecture in London and returned to Waterford around 1744. His input to the Bishop's Palace in 1745 was pivotal to his career, and numerous commissions followed. In subsequent years, Roberts designed and built most of the outstanding works of Georgian Waterford. These included the Leper Hospital (1785), Faithlegg House for Cornelius Bolton (1773), Newtown House for John Wyse (1786) and an imposing private residence, with its extraordinary cantilever staircase, for William Morris, one of the city's leading Protestant merchants, at a cost of £10,000. Unfortunately Morris never lived to see the house completed; in 1813 the building was purchased by the Waterford Chamber of Commerce for £2,500 and today it forms the organisation's headquarters. Noted for his integrity, 'Honest John' insisted on paying his workers on Saturday mornings to enable them to benefit from the freshest food and the best prices available at the morning markets. He also insisted on paying half the wages to the workers' wives to reduce the amount available for spending by the workers in Waterford's public houses.

The prosperity Waterford enjoyed during the second half of the eighteenth century meant the alteration of the medieval city continued, with the construction of new and more spacious properties. Roberts' two greatest achievements were the construction of the Protestant and Catholic cathedrals. In 1773 Thomas Ivory conducted a survey of Christ Church Cathedral and recommended that the old building be replaced. Church and corporation authorities engaged in a joint demolition and construction project, and the new church was completed in 1780 at a cost of £5,397, with work on the spire concluded in 1788. The exterior of the present-day cathedral retains much of the original. It is the only Neo-Classical cathedral in Ireland. A fire, which broke out in the organ gallery in 1815, destroyed much of the cathedral's interior along with the magnificent Elliot organ. The cathedral remained closed for three years for repair and reconstruction. On the recommendation of Sir Thomas Drew, in 1891 the square pews and galleries were removed and the ground-floor windows blocked up.

It is a testament to Roberts' esteem that he was also asked to design the Catholic cathedral in Barronstrand Street. This was the first post-Reformation Catholic cathedral constructed in the United Kingdom and gives Waterford the unique distinction of being the only city in Europe where the Catholic and Protestant cathedrals were designed by the same man. The cathedral was Roberts' last great creation and one that he did not live to see completed. His dedication to his work indirectly led to his death. He awoke early one morning and, believing that it was six o'clock, made his way to the cathedral building site. As it was only 3 a.m. there were no workers present and the old architect curled up on the cold ground and fell asleep. The exposure led to Roberts contracting pneumonia and he died on 24 May 1796, aged 82. In 1985, Edward McParland, the biographer of James Gandon, wrote that:

> Waterford more than any other city in the country in the late eighteenth century succeeded in expressing its civic dignity with fitting architectural grandeur ... The density and quality of building in Waterford, however, made the city architecturally pre-eminent. No city of its size had, within its boundaries, as grand a bishop's palace. No eighteenth-century cathedral elsewhere in the country – with the possible exception of Cashel – outdid either of John Roberts's two Waterford cathedrals.

SQUALOR BEHIND THE SPLENDOUR

The Georgian splendour camouflaged the squalor that existed elsewhere in the city, where the mass of the population resided in deplorable conditions. A corporation inspection team reported in 1831 that in Olav's Lane 'some of the poor room-keepers were actually in a state of nudity, and scarcely a particle of furniture to be seen in their apartments; the end of the lane is a reservoir of filth'. 'A large accumulation of dung into which a sewer from Power's yard empties itself' was found in Philip Street; in Morris's Road 'the houses are generally dirty and the back yards are filled with manure and offensive dung. Gut houses are found here'. Houses in Ballybricken 'where no yard is attached, the pig forms one of the family'.

In 1835, John Barrow, an English visitor found the city to be 'a dark dirty mean-looking place, but improves on advancing towards the fine quay'.

Almost a century later very little had changed. Medical inspector Thomas J. Browne reported in June 1900 that 'in the older parts of the city, the labouring classes were accommodated in tenement buildings which were as a rule very filthy and dilapidated structures, badly lighted and ventilated'. Overcrowding was common, although in the outskirts of the city 'the poorer classes were better housed'. Several insanitary districts were identified, characterised by 'overcrowding, filth, dilapidation, and general sanitary defects'. The death rate in 1899 was 26.4 per 1,000, one of the highest for an urban area in the country. Measles, scarlatina, whooping cough, diarrhoea and influenza were present in epidemic form during the year and were partly a product of the 'insanitary conditions under which a considerable proportion of the poorer classes of Waterford lived' and in particular 'the state of the tenement houses, each room of which is generally occupied by a separate family, and the houses being commonly in a state of dilapidation, filthy without a water supply or adequate closet accommodation; the filthy state of the yards, ashpits, and privies; the keeping of pigs in small, confined yards giving rise to nuisances ...'

LATER DEVELOPMENTS

The nineteenth century was one of infrastructural development in the city. The earliest gas lighting was introduced in 1816 by the iron-foundry proprietor Benjamin Graham. The first bridge across the River Suir, a timber toll bridge, affectionately known as Timbertoes, was built in 1794 by the American builder Lemuel Cox at a cost of £14,000 and continued as the main bridge until the bridge and ferry rights were purchased in 1907. In 1911, work began on a 200ft bridge, which was opened by John Redmond in 1913. This event attracted over 25,000 people anxious to get a glimpse of the undisputed leader of nationalist Ireland as his carriage paraded along the Quay, accompanied by several bands while the strains of 'A Nation Once Again' echoed down the streets. The bridge was subsequently named the John Redmond Bridge. It was, the *Munster Express* reported, 'a stirring spectacle and one the like of which will not be again witnessed in Waterford for many a day to come'.

In 1982 work began on the construction of a new bridge across the River Suir at Waterford after the Redmond Bridge was deemed unsafe and the first two lanes of the bridge were officially opened in 1984. The 204-metre wide bridge was officially named the Brother Edmund Ignatius Rice Bridge.

Waterford was the only city apart from Dublin with five separate railway lines. The first to be completed was the Limerick–Waterford line and this was followed by connections with Dublin via Kilkenny, Cork via Mallow and with Rosslare. A short independent line linked Waterford with the seaside resort of Tramore.

Social provision was of little interest to the municipal authorities. In the forty years prior to independence fewer than twelve working-class houses were built by Waterford Corporation annually, despite the fact that 20 per cent of the city's working-class families lived in city-centre tenements. Almost 80 per cent of the working-class houses were single-storey cottages, the majority occupied by more than one family. Between 1891 and 1911 the number of houses decreased by fifty-eight whilst the city population increased by over 1,000 to 27,464. This was to change in the post-independence decades as the corporation constructed 756 working-class houses extending outwards from Ballybricken. The first houses with indoor toilets were built in 1938 at St Carthage's Avenue. The largest post-war scheme was built at St John's Park, where the first thirty houses were reserved for Waterford Glass workers.

The 1960s witnessed something of an industrial boom leading to rural to urban migration and led to the city expanding westwards. The third-level Waterford Institute of Technology was established in 1970 and the Waterford Regional Hospital, a teaching hospital, in 1987. The city centre was also transformed and pedestrianised in the 1980s and 1990s, a development driven by the tax-driven urban renewal schemes introduced by successive Irish governments.

3

SMALL TOWN WATERFORD

Ireland's urban history is represented in a micro setting in Waterford. The county has an extraordinary urban history with a wide variety of urban types that range in origin from ninth-century monasteries to the mid-nineteenth-century industrial village. This chapter identifies some of the key formative influences of the urban centres of the county.

BUNMAHON: A NINETEENTH-CENTURY MINING SETTLEMENT

R.H. Ryland, in his history of Waterford published in 1824, was taken by the picturesque appearance of Bunmahon. Bunmahon 'consisted of some handsome private residences and several convenient lodging houses generally occupied during the summer season'. 'A popular and fashionable bathing place; a circular race course, a convenient strand and public rooms' were listed as the village's attractions.

Ryland's observations were made at a pivotal time in Bunmahon's history, when the Mining Company of Ireland (MCI) discovered sufficient veins of copper in the Knockmahon district to justify commercial exploitation. The infrastructure of an extractive industry was carved into the rural landscape and included the sinking of shafts, the construction of winding gear, excavating tunnels and ventilation shafts. Over 12 miles of water channels were built to divert water to the area in order to create the energy necessary to turn the 40ft waterwheel and three smaller wheels that were central to the system. In the mid-1830s, steam power replaced water. Coal was imported from Swansea and the copper produced by the mine provided the schooners with cargo for the return journey. As Bunmahon did not have a harbour, the ore was transported in rowing boats to the offshore schooners. Ore production averaged 7,500 tons in the late 1830s and early 1840s, production values that required about seventy-five shipments annually.

In 1841, the mines employed approximately 1,100 men, women and children. Expertise was imported, mainly from Cornwall, but the bulk of the workforce was local. Extracting the ore was extremely dangerous work and strictly the preserve of adult males. It was usually contracted to teams, the number on the teams depending on the distance the ore had to be transported underground. Prior to the closure in 1849, work at the Knockmahon mine was carried out at a depth of 1,000m with the ore face located 250m from the base of the entry shaft. The rock was broken by controlled explosions using gunpowder fired by lighted fuses. The ore-bearing rock was then loaded into wagons and pushed back to the main shaft, where the wagons were emptied into large iron buckets and drawn to the surface. The rock was then transported by horse and cart to the dressing sheds for sorting. This was women's work: the stronger girls hammered rock pieces from the ore and carried the ore to the grinding area where it was reduced to fine sand. This was a mechanical operation, a process that gradually removed the non-metallic material from the ore which was then bagged for export.

Margaret Gough, a fifteen-year-old girl who was employed in the mines, was interviewed by Frederick Roper, a government-appointed inspector of mines, in May 1841. Her testimony provides a graphic insight into conditions at the time:

> I have been working here for these three years. I have always worked at picking; I get 4d a day. I like my work very well. It is not hard work. We have to sit down at our work, and always work under a shed. I have never been to school. I cannot either read or write. I have three brothers and five sisters. They are all at home. Two of them besides me work here. We are very poor. I have no shoes or other clothes than these I have on. I can sew a little. I get paid very regularly. I give my wages to my mother.

Thomas Maher, a thirteen-year-old boy who was employed at budling, informed Roper that 'we sometimes get a cut with a stick if we are not attentive'. Maher had never been to school and existed on a diet of potatoes and 'sometimes a bit of fish'; eleven-year-old Maurice Cuddy had already been employed for three years at the mines; he too worked at budling and also at 'keeping back the skimmings at one of the washings'. An illiterate who never attended school, he informed Roper that 'some of us get a slap of the head sometimes, or a cut with a stick, when not attentive to our work'. Roper reported that the potential for further employment was undermined by the difficulty in recruiting more children to work. Management was unable to do this 'because they have so much trouble with the children and the young persons already employed' as there was 'great difficulty in getting [them] to come to work at all'. They were 'irregular in their attendance, very averse to work, and will not come when the weather is unfavourable ...'

The town of Bunmahon rapidly expanded and its population increased from 357 people in 1821 to 1,771 in 1841. Over the same period the number of houses only increased from 76 to 158. A report in 1832 recorded that as a 'consequence of the daily influx of miners' Bunmahon 'was crowded to excess to such an extent that few rooms contain less than three or four families'. Almost ninety of the houses were one-roomed cabins, many scattered through the sand dunes where shanty town-like living conditions existed.

Disposable income, the dangers and drudgery associated with the industry and the overcrowding encouraged heavy drinking as an escape mechanism. By the late 1830s alcohol abuse was a serious problem in Bunmahon. According to a *Waterford Chronicle* report in 1839, 3,000 barrels of beer and an equal amount of whiskey were annually consumed in the town. The police were required to close all public houses on Sunday mornings to preserve law and order, despite the fact that drinking on a Sunday was a reserved sin in the diocese of Waterford and Lismore for Catholics from which absolution could only be obtained from a bishop.

The late 1830s–early 1840s are associated with the temperance movement headed by the Capuchin priest Fr Theobald Mathew. Waterford had its own temperance zealot, Fr John Foley, a native of Clashmore who trained for the priesthood in both Spain and Paris, where he was ordained in 1815. Foley, 'learned, austere, and rigorously abstemious', was appointed a curate in Youghal from where he began his temperance crusade in 1839. The miners of Bunmahon attracted Fr Foley's attention and in November 1839 it was reported that all the miners pledged to abstain from liquor. However, the adoption of this new lifestyle was not totally voluntary; by June 1840 a vigilante-type six-man 'moral police force' was established to enforce conformity amongst the miners. Not only were miners forbidden to drink but visits to any shop where drink was sold were also excluded. The activities of the miners on Sundays and paydays were observed. Superstition, dismissal from the mines, censure from the pulpit and withholding of the sacraments were used as deterrents and punishments to promote temperance as management and the parish curate, Fr James Power, joined forces in a mutually beneficial crusade. Given the combination of factors at work it was no great surprise that the temperance movement in Bunmahon was a great success. A new Temperance Hall costing £1,000 was built from contributions collected locally (£400) and in the USA by Fr James Power (£600). The impact was immediate: productivity increased and mining manager John Petherick reported that in 1841 the same number of people were earning £300 per month more than they had been doing the previous year. Unfortunately the good times were not to last.

The mines in Knockmahon experienced the classic problems of the industry during the second half of the 1840s. With the most accessible ore extracted, the viable seams were now fractured and at great depths and the flooding of the tunnels became a problem. In 1848 and 1849, the price of copper on the international market fluctuated and eventually declined. In 1846 and 1847, the mining enterprise barely turned a profit and became a loss-making venture in the 1848–1850 period. Unfortunately this collapse coincided with the years of the Great Famine. This posed severe difficulties for Bunmahon, reflected in the town's 35 per cent population decline between 1841 and 1851. Inevitably, the poorest suffered the most. The shanty town with 129 families in ninety houses was reduced to eighteen families who lived in fourteen houses in 1851.

In the early 1850s, mining switched to the Tankardstown region and close to £10,000 was invested in sinking the main shaft to a depth of 100m and in constructing a railway from the Tankardstown storage yard to the dressing sheds. The venture was a success and profits and production soared, peaking in the early 1860s. The area was transformed into a significant industrial development with seven engine houses and two new waterwheels added to the four in action at the dressing rooms. In July 1860, the mines experienced their first strike; company directors responded by closing the business and initiated a lockout that lasted for three-weeks. Problems began when the MCI ended its policy of paying miners for discovering new veins of ore; the method of paying the miners with company tokens redeemable only at the company shop was also a source of annoyance. The directors were uncompromising and after three weeks the miners began to drift back to work. New working arrangements were implemented, unproductive parts of the mine were closed and on resumption productivity declined but profits increased. In 1863, MCI earned £10,000 from its Bunmahon operations. The highest profits ever recorded for the Tankardstown mine, £12,000, were achieved during the first six months of 1865 but, ominously, the profit margin dropped to below £6,000 for the second half of the year. The value of MCI shares more than halved over the course of the year and the trend was to continue. The quality of the ore deteriorated and the rock at depths of up to 200m was harder to exploit. Fluctuations in the price of copper added to Tankardstown's vulnerability. Attempts to find new orebodies in the district were unsuccessful and the railway from Tankardstown was dismantled in 1876. At the end of 1877 the water pumps were removed, effectively decommissioning the mines, and in 1878 the miners' cottages were demolished. In 1879 MCI's lease lapsed. Since 1876, there have been a number of false dawns but, apart from a brief interlude in 1905–06, whatever copper ore is lying underground in Bunmahon has remained undisturbed.

The population of the town declined sharply from 1,343 in 1861 to 320 in 1881 and to just 176 people in 1891. 'It was as if an angel of death had swept over Bunmahon', one contemporary report observed. An even starker picture is revealed when the townlands of Tankardstown and Knockmahon are factored into the population equation where the decline was from 2,059 in 1861 to just 368 in 1881.

DUNGARVAN: THE LANDLORD AS AN AGENT OF URBAN IMPROVEMENT

Dungarvan's urban origins are uncertain. The town may have developed in association with a monastery founded by St Garvin in the seventh century but there is no direct historical evidence to validate this. What is certain is that Dungarvan's development correlated with the English advance in County Waterford. A substantial stone castle was built around 1185 to command the natural harbour at the mouth of the Colligan River.

At the beginning of the nineteenth century Dungarvan was in an advanced state of decay; a town 'fully deserving of the reproachful epithets which travellers universally bestowed upon it', according to R.H. Ryland.

> The streets and buildings were of the most wretched description and continued in the same state until a few years since. Crowded with miserable houses, irregular in appearance, without any or at all events an inefficient police ... There were no regular market-places, no public water works: the court-house ... was considered unsafe for the purposes for which it was originally intended: there was no bridge, and consequently no way of passing from the town to the Waterford side of the river except by ferry boat, or, as was generally the case with the lower classes, by fording the stream at low water.

In addition unemployment was common, the fisheries were neglected and the 'prisons were a disgrace to a civilized country'.

This was the extent of the decay facing the Dukes of Devonshire when they made their radical transforming intervention in the town's urban landscape during the opening decades of the 1800s.

In 1748, the Devonshire family inherited extensive landed estates in counties Cork and Waterford, an inheritance that included 28 acres of Dungarvan land, most of it located outside the town walls. In 1775, the 5th Duke of Devonshire commissioned Bernard Scalé to map his estates. Scalé reported that the duke's Dungarvan property consisted of the poorest category of cabins built around the edge of large communal gardens. In 1794, the duke's houses were described as being 'built of mud, covered in straw, mostly old'.

The passing of the Act of Union in 1801 boosted its political importance. The act reduced the number of parliamentary seats from over 200 to 100, which were transferred to the parliament in Westminster. Dungarvan held one of the thirty-three borough seats that survived the cull until 1833, a development that was not lost on the duke or his political advisers. Dungarvan was one of the five post-Union boroughs with a property-based franchise. Only householders with property valued at more than £5 annually and freeholders in the manor worth more than 40s were enfranchised, and unfortunately for the Duke of Devonshire the majority of his tenants were impoverished fishermen who were ineligible to vote.

Following the defeat of the duke's candidate at the 1802 general election his agent, Thomas Knowlton, initiated an urban improvement programme, funded by the duke, that transformed

Dungarvan and was designed to boost the duke's image and reflect favourably on his political nominee. This began with what was essentially a slum clearance programme. In the period 1802–1806, Devonshire Square (now Grattan Square), Bridge Street, Cross Bridge Street and William Street (now St Mary's Street) were laid out and contracts agreed for building houses along them. The intervention was also successful politically as in the general election of 1806 the duke's nominee, General George Walpole, was elected. The Devonshire's programme of urban renewal continued and between 1803 and 1830 over £71,000 was invested in Dungarvan. A site for the Catholic church was gifted and a donation of £1,500 was made to help with building costs; a bridge over the River Colligan was constructed between 1810 and 1816 to the design of William Atkenson, at the sole expense of the duke, and new quays were constructed in the late 1820s. Between 1811 and 1830, close to 400 small freeholders' cabins were built on the southern edge of the town at Blackpool and Boreheenatra. Each cabin was leased for the duration of the life of one named elderly person. All of this, as L.J. Proudfoot has pointed out, was 'for the express purpose of increasing the number of voters who would support the duke's candidate'. The intervention was a success and the duke retained political control of the borough until 1832, when he withdrew from active involvement in Irish politics.

As a result of the Devonshires' urban improvement scheme, R.H. Ryland was able to deliver a positive verdict on the Dungarvan of 1824: 'Dungarvan is now a handsome and certainly an improving town'.

In 1858, the 6th Duke of Devonshire died, leaving behind debts of over £1 million. As part of a retrenchment programme, the family sold their Dungarvan interests to the sitting tenants for a sum of £29,000 between 1859 and 1861. The Devonshire association with the town was thus ended but the urbanscape of present-day Dungarvan is essentially the creation of the 5th and 6th Dukes of Devonshire, their agents and architects. The town experienced little growth until the 2000s. Pre-Famine Dungarvan had a population of 8,625 but by 1851 this had fallen to 6,311. This decline continued and by 1901 the town was home to 4,977 people, by 2011 it housed 7,991 people.

PORTLAW: A NINETEENTH-CENTURY PLANNED INDUSTRIAL VILLAGE

Few Irish towns are comparable to Portlaw, a purpose-built industrial village constructed to accommodate the workers of David Malcomson's cotton factory on the banks of the River Clodiagh. The original town was built between 1825 and 1850; the core Malcomson development consisted of the parallel streets of Mulgrave Street and Shamrock Street. A second Malcomson development, Green Island, was located between the canal and the River Clodiagh, whilst Queen Street formed the eastern boundary of the town.

'Portlaw in Ireland afforded far better and more comfortable accommodation than, so far as I have observed, is to be found for any other of the working population in any other parts of Scotland or Ireland', factory inspector James Stewart reported in 1842. Mr and Mrs Hall were in Portlaw the same year and they noted that 'The houses are clean and comfortable, the people are all decently dressed; there is an air of improvement in everything that pertains to them'.

Apart from high-quality housing, the Malcomson enterprise at Portlaw supported a wide range of social facilities. Health and welfare were catered for by the dispensary and from 1835 by the resident factory surgeon, Dr James Martin. A fever hospital was also under the supervision of Dr Martin and was supported jointly by the Malcomson firm and workers' contributions. The Mayfield Providence Society administered a form of social insurance that provided financial support to subscribing members in the event of illness. A variety of methods were used to vigorously promote temperance. The Portlaw Tontine Club was established in 1838 with the dual purpose of promoting temperance and the habit of saving. A member subscribed weekly to a savings fund and at the end of a defined period the capital, with interest, was divided between the subscribers. However, any member convicted of intoxication or of giving or taking drink in a public house within 4 miles of his own residence was expelled from the society without recompense.

Education was one of the key social provisions supported by the Malcomson family, and in the 1850s they invested £2,000 in constructing a school designed by John Skipton Mulvany, one of the leading architects of the time. In 1868 the firm estimated that their annual contribution to education amounted to £200. From 1855 onwards, separate male, female, infants and evening schools were established and affiliated to the national Board of Education.

By the late 1850s the original Portlaw development had outlived its usefulness and the proprietors radically intervened to transform the urbanscape based on a unitary design plan. The parallel Mulgrave and Shamrock Streets were demolished and replaced by an original trivium-shaped formal design, which was recognised as one of the most significant aspects of Portlaw's design in the Heritage Conservation Plan of 2003.

The revolutionary intervention began with the construction of a terrace of fifty two-storey houses on the south side of Brown Street, completed by 1859. By August 1861, it was reported that the factory proprietors had

> Taken down nearly all the old houses and erected good roomy comfortable houses to the number of about 120, and are continuing to work at the erection of at least as many more, with large windows, provision for the separation of the sexes, and other appliances for comfort and decency.

Much of the development was completed by 1867, including the sixty-three houses of William Street and the fifty-five houses of George's Street. These were single-storey three-bay, four-room houses, with an entrance directly into the front room and three rooms opening off this room, one to the front and two to the rear, divided by a hallway. The high construction standards used in these buildings is emphasised by the fact that many are still inhabited and structurally sound. Construction followed a uniform pattern. The outside walls were stone and rendered with lime plaster; the dividing walls were of brick. Bedroom floors were boarded and those of the kitchen and passages asphalted. Each room had a fireplace and chimney and each kitchen included a range with an oven and side tank for hot water. Each house had an enclosed backyard with a dry toilet and small back garden.

The roofs were the most distinctive architectural feature of the development. In Portlaw, the use of the prefabricated, curved trellised softwood-frame roof trusses was a key design feature.

The framework, designed to provide substantial overhanging eaves, was then covered with several layers of tarred calico. Both the frames and covering material were manufactured at the cotton factory and this allowed a 50 per cent reduction in the cost of roofing the Portlaw houses compared to using conventional slate roofs. The dwellings cost £40 to construct with the total Malcomson investment in housing estimated at £10,000 in 1871. The completed development, with its triangular pattern of street plan, regular plots, straight and wide streets and the similarity of house design, generated in Portlaw a sense of uniformity, spaciousness and order that was rare in a small Irish town.

The redevelopment of the town was motivated by a variety of social and economic factors. Despite the favourable response of contemporary visitors, the quality of housing failed to meet the exacting standards required by the Malcomson family. It was also overcrowded. The population of Portlaw increased by 19 per cent during the 1840s. According to the census of 1851, 245 families were squashed into 137 second-class houses and 688 families occupied 364 third-class houses. The period of reconstruction coincided with a period of great economic success for the Malcomson business. Confidence was high and housing developments at Portlaw were a visible expression of this confidence. The development of housing stock was also a sound economic investment that offered the prospect of a rapid return. Tenants and rental returns were guaranteed as long as the Portlaw enterprise remained viable.

William Malcomson was the chief partner of the firm when much of the radical intervention took place. His Quaker-inspired principles of concern for his fellow man and a belief in the practical benefits to be gained from taking proper care of a labour force were also important in inspiring the remodelling.

Unfortunately the good times were not to last; in 1876 the Malcomson business empire was declared bankrupt with disastrous consequences for Portlaw. In 1900, uninhabited houses, partly deserted streets, economic stagnation and decay defined the once-showpiece industrial village. Economic migration meant that between 1871 and 1901 the population declined from 3,774 to 1,101, the sharpest decline taking place between 1871 and 1881 when the population dropped by 1,883. In 1900, David Wark, a Presbyterian minister from Waterford city, visited Portlaw and 'found a general air of decay' throughout. The village that attracted such favourable comment in earlier decades was now a place with

> Long rows of houses, with windows boarded up, and stuck over with a patchwork of advertisements in various stages of decay, or with gaping holes where the glass has been broken away, while off the outsides the plaster has fallen in great patches giving the walls the appearance of having been attacked by some devastating skin disease.

After more than thirty years as an economic wasteland, Portlaw experienced a revival in the early 1930s when the firm Irish Tanners Ltd opened and provided industrial employment until it closed its doors in 1985.

TRAMORE: THE SEASIDE RESORT

According to the *Parliamentary Gazetteer of Ireland*, Tramore in 1846 was 'incompact and straggling; but on that very account, possesses superior adaption to its uses as a sea bathing resort and it has long been the favourite retreat of the citizens of Waterford and the inhabitants of the circumadjacent country'. Since the eighteenth century, tourism has been the engine that has driven Tramore's development and economy. Bartholomew Rivers was the driving force behind Tramore's transformation from fishing village to recreational centre. He was one of Waterford's most successful merchants, a ship owner, a porter and spirits seller, wine importer, a wholesale-grocery proprietor, a dealer in imported luxury goods such as hops, teas, sugars and spices, as well as a banker. In 1778, he moved to Tramore and began to promote the village as a seaside resort, encouraging the wealthy to reside there or visit. By 1824 Tramore had developed into a 'neat, well-built village' and by 1831 its population had grown to 2,214. Mr and Mrs S.C. Hall, in their 1840s visit, noted that 'of late years several capital houses have been built there, and it wears a prosperous aspect'.

Racing and hunting were central to the recreational culture of the landed gentry and the fulcrum about which a variety of other activities revolved. The poor also attended racing in great numbers as the entry was free and a range of ancillary entertainment was available. Bartholomew Rivers is credited with introducing the sport to Tramore, building an embankment at the Back Strand on which races were staged in 1785, 1793, 1795 and 1797. In August 1807 a six-day meet was staged. Racing declined in the 1860s and 1870s, but in the late 1870s a new, almost perfectly level one-mile track and a stand house capable of holding 2,000 people were constructed. The course's location on the reclaimed and protected back strand made it vulnerable and on 13 December 1911 the racecourse was flooded beyond repair. A new course was developed at Graun Hill, which opened for business in 1912 and where racing has been almost ever-present since.

On 1 January 2002 Tramore was the first racecourse in Europe to use the Euro currency and on that date in 2000 it held the first race meeting of the new millennium in Europe, which was attended by a record crowd of 11,000. The first race of the millennium, The Mean Fiddler Handicap Steeplechase, was won by No Problem, trained in Cork by Gerard Cully, owned by Tommy Cronin and ridden by Waterford jockey Shay Barry.

Golf was also an attraction and in 1894 Tramore Golf Club was formed; it became affiliated to the Golfing Union of Ireland in 1896. The great storm of 1911 also destroyed the golf links and forced the members to relocate inland.

In 1895, aware of the need to diversify the range of attractions, Martin J. Murphy invited Mr Toft to bring his fairground to the village. The experiment was so successful that Toft donated an evening's takings on the merry-go-round to help pay for a boat to rescue swimmers. Mr Beach provided the entertainment in 1900; Bill Piper married Emily Beach and this alliance began an unbroken Piper association with Tramore's amusements. In 1908, Piper's attractions included a South African farmyard (which enabled patrons to ride on an ostrich, a camel, or some other exotic bird or animal), galloping horses, love-in-a-tub, pipe breakers, swing boats and the helter-skelter lighthouse imported directly from Coney Island.

Johnny McGurk opened his Marquee de Danse and purchased the Sierra Leone Palace at the Wembley Exhibition in 1924 and had it erected in Tramore in time for the August Racing Festival of 1926. The Palace Ballroom served as a multipurpose venue and was used as a cinema, dance hall and skating rink for the entrepreneurial McGurk.

Tramore's fortunes as a tourist centre received a considerable boost when the Waterford–Tramore railway opened on 5 September 1853 and made Tramore accessible to the day visitor. It also helped to establish Tramore as a dormitory town for the wealthy of Waterford city. On the opening day the company directors and 200 guests were carried from Waterford to Tramore. Two days later over 5,000 passengers made the journey and at one point the police had to be called to maintain law and order, such was the clamour to make the fifteen-minute journey to Tramore. The line was the only independent one in the country. The national lines offered special rates to Tramore and people from all over Ireland availed of the opportunity to visit; in the 1890s the Great Southern and Western Line offered weekend and tourist fares from thirty-seven different stations ranging from Sligo and Tralee to Tramore, advertised as 'the Brighton of Ireland' and a place 'specially adapted to invalids on account of the mildness of the climate and is deservedly one of the most popular summer resorts'. Tramore hotel proprietors and the railway directors combined to offer attractive packets to potential tourists at discounted rates. The rail company also encouraged settlement in Tramore by carrying building materials free of charge and those relocating were provided with free first-class travel for five years.

LISMORE: A CAVENDISH FAMILY CREATION

Lismore's settlement has a number of distinct phases, beginning with the monastic settlement established by St Carthage. By the mid-1750s Lismore was a derelict town. In 1746 Charles Smith noted that 'instead of its ancient lustre, the cathedral, castle and a few tolerable houses intertwixt with cabins are all that now appear'. In the 1790s, the Devonshire agent Henry Bowman reported that 'At present the town (a few houses excepted) is almost in ruins'. Most of the town's houses were straw-covered mud cabins. Bowman had ambitious plans for Lismore and placed particular emphasis on improving the town's communications as a means of driving its economy. He planned to construct a canal linking Lismore and Youghal via the Blackwater River, a road across the Knockmealdown Mountains to improve access with County Tipperary and develop direct road links between the town and Cork city. He also planned to construct a new inn and to progressively reconstruct the town's entire housing stock. The inn, the canal and a road to Clogheen, County Tipperary were completed between 1793 and 1797, when Bowman resigned his post. The inn, 'a substantial four-storey Georgian building', survives and today trades as the Lismore Hotel. It is one of the town's dominant buildings and claims to be the first purpose-built hotel in Ireland. Unfortunately, despite Bowman's best ambitions, the completion of the canal in 1796 had little impact on the town's or estate's economy and plans for the estate were disrupted by the tensions and economic difficulties associated with the 1798 rebellion.

William Cavendish, the 6th Duke of Devonshire, invested heavily in improving his Irish estates and the town's present-day morphology is essentially his creation; between 1820 and 1822 Lismore was remodelled and rebuilt when the Green, the North and South Malls, New Street and West Street were laid out. 'Poor peoples' houses' on Gallow's Hill were demolished and the occupants rehoused in purpose-built houses on West Street. A new road was built from the bridge to the town, sewers were laid, cabins along Chapel Lane were demolished and in 1823–24 Chapel Place was constructed and connected Chapel Lane with the South Mall. This was the last major addition to the street plan in Lismore during the 1820s building campaign. Later estate-financed construction concentrated on minor infrastructural improvements and in building additional artisans' houses in New Street and at the north end of Chapel Lane. The seventy-five houses of New Street were built between 1823 and 1832; the construction of houses on Chapel Lane was a slower process and its fifty-five habitations were not completed until around 1840. This did not end the duke's investment in Lismore and he later financed the construction of various public utilities, including the town's gas supply and its first public water supply as well as the construction of a new bridge in 1856 to replace Thomas Ivory's collapsed late eighteenth-century bridge. The Duke's impact in Lismore Casle is examined in Chapter 5.

TALLOW: THE MUNSTER PLANTATION TOWN

Tallow's origins lie in the Munster Plantation. A 'decayed town' and its surrounding lands was granted to Sir Walter Raleigh in 1586 and, like Lismore, it was subsequently transferred to Sir Richard Boyle and eventually became part of the Cavendish portfolio and the finest urban property of the estate. It received its charter from James I in 1614 and became a parliamentary borough, returning two members to the Irish Parliament until the passing of the Act of Union in 1801. Tallow developed as one of the principal English settlements of the Munster Plantation and by 1662 consisted of around 150 English households with a possible population of 750 people. The two main streets, formed at the junction of the main road from Lismore to Youghal and Midleton to Cork, gave the town a cruciform plan. The town developed around the market house and the central market place and along West Street and in 1800 consisted of slate houses with extensive stores. In 1794 Henry Bowman described it as 'more extensive than Lismore, better built and at present [has] a better share of trade'; in 1831 it consisted of 477 houses of which 'many are well built and of respectable appearance', a significant increase from the 266 houses recorded in 1776.

Tallow's economic success was directly connected to its links to the outside world. The River Bride was navigable to the town and provided a transport link with Youghal via the Blackwater. At Janeville Quay, 2 miles outside the town, and Tallow Bridge

Quay lighters of 30–40-ton capacity brought cargoes of coal and timber from Youghal and transported grain from Fermoy and the neighbouring markets. The wool-combing business provided Tallow's initial prosperity; in the 1840s the manufacture of coarse lace provided employment for several hundred women and in 1835 a brewery was established, producing 3,000 barrels of beer annually, in association with a large malting concern. Hannan's waterpower-driven flour mills were established in 1822 and in the mid-1830s produced 10,000 barrels of flour annually. Consequently Tallow required little Cavendish investment but the estate financed the installation of the public water supply and relayed the sewage system in the town during the 1860s.

OTHER PLACES

Other urban-village settlements also developed in the county. Cappoquin, of medieval origins, was the only significant west-Waterford urban settlement that was not part of the Cavendish estate. It was a post town, chiefly associated in the mid-nineteenth century with Sir Richard Keane who occupied 'a handsome mansion of hewn stone, situated in a richly improved, and well planted demesne, commanding a fine view of Dromona and the river Blackwater'. Keane at one stage resided in France and provided 600 acres of rent-free land on the slopes of the Knockmealdown Mountains to a group of Cistercian monks who were expelled from France and who established their monastery, Mount Mellary, there in 1835.

A desire for improvement was one of the defining characteristics of the eighteenth century and in 1731 the Dublin Society was established for 'improving husbandry, manufacture and the useful arts and sciences'. Lord Grandison was a member and in the 1750s he developed Villierstown on the edge of his Dromana estate as 'a new and neat colony erected for the advancement of the Linen Manufacture'. Villierstown was built to a formal plan with the church in the centre and a wide main street flanked by plain stone buildings.

Other settlements failed to progress beyond the planning stage. New Geneva, designed by James Gandon to house religious refugees from Geneva with a central Temple Square, wide streets, a market, prison, hospital and school, never progressed beyond the laying of the foundation in July 1784 and the construction of some buildings around the central square. It was planned that 11,000 acres close to Passage East would be colonised by over 1,000 refugees who were skilled artisans, and that their skills would transfer to the natives – as Lord Temple, the lord lieutenant, explained, 'they might make an essential reform in the religion, industry and manners of the south'. The Irish Parliament granted £50,000 towards the project. However, Lord Temple, the passionate promoter of the project, was replaced and his successors did not share his enthusiasm. The few buildings that were constructed were converted to a military barracks, which was abandoned in 1824.

Nearby Dunmore East 'was originally a poor fishing village, consisting of only a few cabins built of clay, and thatched with straw'. Its fortunes were transformed by the government decision to make it one of four stations in Ireland for the mail packets from Milford Haven. A new pier, quay, breakwater and harbour, government funded to the sum of £108,286, were built to the design of Alexander Nimmo, between 1814 and 1841. Four steamers served the Dunmore–Milford route. Dunmore Harbour House was built to meet the needs of travellers. Dunmore East's function as a fishing village continued and with the harbour improvements it became 'a fashionable bathing-place', with its thatched cottages 'let to visitors during the season'.

4

ROYAL VISITS

THE ENGLISH TAKE OVER

Waterford's location at the head of a superb natural harbour at the mouth of three navigable rivers, the Suir, Nore and Barrow, which are tidal for several miles upriver and its proximity to Bristol and France gave the city a distinct advantage over almost all other Irish ports.

In the years between 1169 and 1171 Ireland was invaded and a large part of the island was brought under English control. Their arrival was connected to the internal politics of the kingdom of Leinster. In 1165 Diarmait Mac Murchadha lost out in his struggles with Tigernán ua Ruairc, King of Breifne, and Ruadhrí Ó Conchobair, King of Connacht for control of Dublin and the southeast of Ireland. Mac Murchadha immediately set sail for Bristol where he checked in with his friend Robert fitz Harding, who advised him to seek the support of King Henry II, the most powerful monarch in western Europe and ruler of England, Normandy, Brittany, Anjou, Aquitaine and most of Wales.

Henry had his own pressures at the time and was unable to offer Diarmait direct assistance. Instead he cleared Diarmait to recruit mercenaries from within his empire to support him in his attempts to regain his power. Mac Murchadha returned to Wales, offered land and money in return for military support and recruited Richard de Clare, Earl of Pembroke (or Strongbow to give him his more popular identity). Strongbow was not the type of mercenary Henry had in mind: he did not come cheaply and in return for his support, Strongbow demanded the hand of Diarmait Mac Murchadha's daughter, Aoife, in marriage and the right to succeed Diarmait as King of Leinster. Leading members of the Fitzgerald family were also recruited in return for the promise of the town of Wexford and surrounding lands.

In 1170 Strongbow set sail from Milford Haven and landed at Passage, County Waterford, on the River Suir estuary in August of the same year with a force of 200 knights and about 1,000 others. From there they marched on Waterford and found the city's gates closed against them. They were joined by Raymond le Gros, who led a party of forty or so knights from their base at Baginbun, County Wexford, and together they attacked the city. They failed twice to breach the city walls but then, according to Gerald of Wales, the main chronicler of the events, Raymond 'noticed a small building which hung down from the town wall on the outside by a beam. He quickly sent in armed men to cut down the aforesaid beam. The building immediately collapsed and with it a considerable part of the wall. The invaders ... rushed into the city and won a most bloody victory, large amounts of the citizens being slaughtered in the streets'. An English garrison secured the city and the English invading party marched on.

HENRY II

Diarmait Mac Murchadha died in May 1171 and Strongbow, who had married Mac Murchadha's daughter in battle-torn Waterford on 25 August 1170, became King of Leinster. The political implications of Strongbow's elevation to the Leinster title were significant and alarmed King Henry II. His newfound standing as King of Leinster, along with his continued base in Wales, provided a potential challenge to Henry's own position. Henry therefore made plans for a full-scale invasion of Ireland and assembled his expeditionary force at Pembroke in October 1171. He paid a visit to the shrine of St David and, spiritually fortified, set sail on 16 October 1171. The following day his fleet of 400 ships, 500 knights and 4,000 foot soldiers, which included a large body of archers, entered Waterford Harbour and anchored at Crooke near Passage East. On St Luke's Day, 18 October 1171, Henry II and his massive army marched on Waterford city. This was the first occasion an English king visited an Irish city and the visit was politically successful. The Irish kings had never seen an army of such might and equipment and had no intention of testing its efficiency.

Diarmait MacCarthy, King of Desmond was the first in a succession of important Irish political leaders who pledged homage to Henry II and acknowledged him as Lord of Ireland during his six months in the country. Anglo-Norman lords also submitted to Henry. Robert Fitzstephen, one of the original English lords recruited by Diarmait Mac Murchadha, was imprisoned by Henry in Reginald's Tower, thus securing another distinction for the iconic building. It became the first prison established in Ireland by the King of England.

Waterford and its hinterland was one of the three areas retained by Henry as part of his royal demesnes; he divided the adjacent territories among his barons to be held by the feudal tenure of knight service. Waterford city was retained as the property of the king and not one of his vassals. Henry's Irish expedition also restored his standing with the Papacy (lost following the murder of Thomas Becket) as he convinced the Papal legates that his Irish expedition was inspired by a desire to reform the Irish Church. He claimed he was acting on a Papal Bull, *Laudabiliter*, issued by Pope Adrian IV back in 1155, which granted him the right to invade and govern Ireland in order to enforce the Gregorian Reforms on the semi-independent Church in Ireland. Within days of Henry's arrival in Waterford, Irish bishops assembled in the cathedral and pledged their support for the reform of the Irish Church.

JOHN

Almost forty years after King Henry's all-conquering visit to Ireland, Waterford had its second royal visit in 1210 when, on 20 June, Henry's son King John sailed into Waterford Harbour with the then largest army ever to arrive in Ireland. It was John's second visit to Waterford as he had also been in the city as an eighteen-year-old prince in 1185, when, according to Gerald of Wales, several Irish chieftains 'greeted him as their lord and received him with the kiss of peace.' Unfortunately the teenage prince and his friends behaved as teenage boys are wont to do and 'treated them with contempt and derision, and showing them scant respect, pulled some of them about by their beards, which were large and flowing according to the native culture,' behaviour that alienated potential supporters both Irish and English. John became seriously ill at one stage during his stay in Waterford and feared that he had contracted leprosy. As he prayed for his recovery, he promised the Lord that if he survived he would build a leper hospital. He made a full recovery and proved to be a youth of his word, building a leper hospital in Waterford dedicated to St Stephen. John endowed the hospital with a large grant of land, the rents of which supported the institution. To this day, these lands, in Dunmore East, are known as Leperstown.

John became King of England in 1199; in the years since 1169 English barons had become rich and powerful in Ireland, especially Strongbow's son-in-law William the Marshal who inherited Leinster to add to his estates in Wales and Normandy and founded the port of New Ross. Theobald Walter was another powerful baron who conquered much of Kilkenny and Tipperary, as was William de Braose, Lord of Limerick, a sworn enemy of King John.

No expense was spared for John's second visit to Ireland, which was inspired by the need to tighten his control over his Irish territories. The army that landed in Crooke, near Passage East, consisted of at least 7,000 knights, archers and foot soldiers as well as craftsmen, labourers and clerks who carried over 600 parchment skins on which to record charters and agreements. It was an extraordinary logistical exercise that involved at least 700 ships. After disembarking at Crooke on 20 June 1210 the party marched to Waterford where King John received the homage of Donough O'Brien, King of Thomond. This trend continued as he moved on to New Ross, Kilkenny and Naas, establishing complete control of the country. In Dublin twenty Irish chiefs paid homage to King John.

A number of towns and cities were granted charters during John's reign. These included Waterford and Dungarvan, which received royal approval on 3 July 1215. For Waterford, it was the first of over thirty charters received over a period of 500 years and contained thirty clauses. The city was established as a distinct administrative unit with a special relationship with the king. The citizens were granted the right to hold their property directly from the king and not from any feudal lord, to manage their own affairs and hold their own courts. They were also free of all taxes on goods bought and sold at fairs or transported by land or water anywhere in King John's realm. Prior to this, in 1204, King John granted the city permission to hold an annual fair during the first eight days of August (this was later extended by a further eight days by Edward I).

This grant was a special privilege intended to attract foreign merchants as those who travelled to and from approved markets were granted royal protection. John also ordered the strengthening of the city's defences and endowed its Benedictine priory.

RICHARD II

Richard II (1377–1399) felt it necessary to visit Ireland in 1394 to reassert his authority. Art Mac Murrough, King of Leinster, provided the greatest threat and from his Wicklow base had been conducting raids on Dublin and Wexford. Waterford was again the chosen port of invasion and on 2 October, after 'only a day and night at sea', Richard arrived in Waterford. He was accompanied by the largest army ever to set foot in Ireland, variously estimated at between 8,000-10,000 men.

At this time, the administration of Ireland was in a shambolic state, and was effective only in a narrow area known as the Pale within a radius of 30 miles of Dublin. Richard remained in Waterford, possibly residing in Greyfriars, until 19 October, awaiting the arrival of his uncle, the Duke of Gloucester. While there, he received homage from his loyal subjects from the surrounding area and prepared his military campaign. Richard's armies crossed the Suir on 19 October and moved into south Kilkenny. Mac Murrough surrendered nine days later. Richard II remained in Ireland for eight months, during which time he attempted to deal with the problems presented by the wild Irish, the Irish rebels and the loyal English. He returned to England on 15 May 1395 and again used the port of Waterford as his point of departure.

Richard's second visit to Waterford in 1399 was brief. Shortly after landing he received news that his cousin, Henry of Bolingbroke, had arrived in England. On his return Richard

RICHARD II.

was imprisoned and forced to abdicate in Henry's favour. He was held prisoner at Pontefract Castle and was either murdered or starved to death, though a legend persisted that he had escaped.

LOYAL WATERFORD

In general terms, Waterford remained loyal to the English monarch for most of its history. This was clearly evident in 1487 when the Earl of Kildare invited Waterford to join him in supporting Lambert Simnel, the pretender to the throne during the first Tudor monarchy, whom he had crowned king in Christ Church Cathedral, Dublin. Despite threats, Waterford remained loyal to Henry VII, the only Irish city to do so. Henry rewarded the city for its loyalty by awarding it a new charter and a grant for the purchase of 200 bows, 400 sheaves of arrows and 400 bow strings.

In 1495, Waterford became the first Irish city to experience an artillery siege when supporters of another pretender, Perkin Warbeck, attacked the city. Warbeck claimed to be the younger brother of the late Edward V and therefore the rightful King of England. He landed at Cork, planning to conquer Ireland before beginning an assault on England. The people that mattered in Dublin as well as the lord deputy supported Warbeck. Waterford again proved to be a stumbling block and on 23 July 1495 Warbeck's forces of 2,500 men, led by the Earls of Lincoln and Desmond, laid siege to the city; the lord mayor, Robert Butler, played the lead role in defending his city. According to a contemporary Waterford account:

> Warbeck's ships drew into Lombard's Weir on the Suir and put down soldiers there. The citizens replied sending a retinue of their own men to attack what they presumed were Rodigue de Lalaing's men. The Flemish were defeated, some were killed outright and some taken prisoner. The prisoners were brought to the city, taken to the market place and beheaded. Thereafter their heads were put on public display ... two of Warbeck's ships were bulged or drowned with ordinance shot out of Dundore [Reginald's Tower].

On 3 August, the siege was lifted as Warbeck's supporters retreated 'with great dishonour and loss'. Waterford had withstood the siege and its status as a favoured royal city was secure and enhanced. It is believed that the city received its motto, *Urbs Intacta Manet Waterfordia* ('the city of Waterford remains untaken'), from Henry VII as a gesture of thanks for its steadfastness against the Warbeck attack. In July 1497, Warbeck returned for another attack on Waterford but this time without a supporting army; a small fleet chased him out of the estuary and pursued him to Cork. Julian Walton has written that defying Warbeck was 'perhaps the most important and triumphant single event in the city's history. It surpassed the protracted and miserable proceedings during the siege by Oliver Cromwell.'

WILLIAM III

Soon after the Battle of the Boyne in July 1690, the victorious King William III travelled south and set up camp beside the river at Carrick-on-Suir. William planned to secure the surrender of Waterford as quickly as possible. General Kirk was dispatched to the city to inform the governor of William's terms for surrender, which included allowing the Jacobite garrison to march to the nearest Jacobite stronghold at Mallow and a promise that the Catholic dwellers of the city would not be 'molested in their properties'. The terms were accepted, the Jacobite garrison departed and General Kirk's army entered the city. Duncannon Fort was also captured. On 26 July 1690, the day after the surrender of Waterford, William made his way down from Carrick-on-Suir and on this inspection visit became the fourth English king to visit the city. According to Waterford folklore, James II also came to the city in 1690, following his defeat at the Battle of the Boyne; he climbed to the top of Reginald's Tower to take a final look at his lost kingdom before embarking for exile in France.

WILLIAM III.

EDWARD VII

The city waited 214 years for the next royal visit. On 2 May 1904 King Edward VII and Queen Alexandra visited Waterford and Lismore. The party arrived at the city's north station shortly after noon and were greeted by the lord mayor, the Duke and Duchess of Devonshire and the Marquis and Marchioness of Waterford. At least ten addresses of welcome were delivered and the South of Ireland Imperial Yeomanry provided the royal escort. The three naval ships in the port, HMS *Melampus,* HMS *Curlew* and HMS *Skipjack*, fired a royal salute when Edward and Alexandra arrived. A procession along the Quay was followed by a luncheon reception in the City Hall. This was followed by a procession through Lombard Street and William Street to St Patrick's Park where the royal party watched a show-jumping competition at the Waterford Agricultural Society Show. The reception was rapturous and the *Munster Express* reported that 'it could scarcely be equalled in enthusiasm' as the strains of 'God Save the King' were 'completely drowned for several minutes by the hearty chorus of cheering which was again and again renewed'. No political significance could be attached to the welcome, as his majesty was greeted more as a declared friend of Ireland and an illustrious sportsman according to the report.

The party departed from the city's south station at 4 p.m. In a dramatic gesture prior to leaving, King Edward VII knighted the Lord Mayor of Waterford, James Power, on the platform. The king and queen spent two nights in Lismore Castle where parties were held each night. On their second day in the west Waterford town, the royal party spent the morning in Lismore before travelling across the Knockmealdown Mountains to visit Lady Pole Carew at Shanbally Castle and Lady Constance Butler at Mountain Lodge.

THE QUEEN OF CAMELOT IN WOODSTOWN

American 'royalty' came calling in June 1967 when the Queen of Camelot, Jacqueline Kennedy, visited Woodstown, County Waterford on a month-long private family vacation. The visit was inspired by a desire to fulfil the wishes of her assassinated husband, John Fitzgerald Kennedy, who enjoyed his 1963 visit to Ireland so much that he promised to return with his wife and children. The assassin's bullet in Dallas, Texas, in November 1963 ended that ambition.

'I am happy to be here in this land that my husband loved so much,' Jacqueline Kennedy announced on arrival at Shannon Airport. When the party reached Woodstown the staff waited in the manner of a royal reception and were somewhat surprised when a gang of noisy children emerged from the Kennedy minibus. Legendary racehorse trainer Phonsie O'Brien was instrumental in finding the Georgian mansion, Woodstown House, for Jacqueline and her friends.

The break for the former US first lady almost ended in tragedy when she got into difficulties while swimming off a secluded beach near the residence. News of the incident did not become public until a letter written by Mrs Kennedy to a Secret Service chief in Washington was published. The combination of cold and a difficult current challenged Kennedy: 'I was becoming exhausted, swallowing water and slipping past the spit of the land, when I felt a great porpoise by my side.' The 'great porpoise' was US Secret Service agent, Jack Walsh, a towering US Marine Corps veteran of the Korean War who came to her rescue and took her ashore. 'Then I sat on the beach coughing up sea water for half an hour while he found a poor itinerant and borrowed a blanket for me,' she wrote.

During her stay, Mrs Kennedy took her children to the Kennedy ancestral home in Dunganstown, County Wexford, and sent them back again the following day to experience the lifestyle of an Irish farm family. Jacqueline Kennedy also officially opened the John F. Kennedy Arboretum in New Ross, County Wexford, visited Lismore Castle, Castletown House, the Waterford Crystal factory, and attended a performance by the Dunhill Players of John B. Keane's play *Many Young Men of Twenty* in the local hall. She was the guest of Taoiseach Jack Lynch at the Irish Sweeps Derby at the Curragh where she saw Lester Piggott steer the American-bred favourite Ribocco, to a one-length victory. In a less intrusive age, the media respected a government request to respect her privacy.

5

WATERFORD'S BUILT HERITAGE

The various influences responsible for shaping the culture of Waterford are reflected in the landscape of the county and in its buildings ranging from the Neolithic through to modern times. Waterford has two of the finest 'big houses' in the country, one of the great gardens of the world (built by Ambrose Congreve), a unique Hindu-Gothic gate lodge and some extraordinary examples of follies. Some of the outstanding features of the county's built heritage are examined in this chapter.

ARDMORE ROUND TOWER AND CATHEDRAL

Modern-day Ardmore has many structures that recognise the town's connection with St Declan. The two most significant, the Round Tower and the ruins of the cathedral, are twelfth-century constructions and are two of Ireland's most important Romanesque monuments. The Round Tower is possibly the last of its kind to be built in Ireland, the earliest examples of which date to the 950s. The tower has an external diameter of 5m at the base, tapering to just over 3m at the top, and it is close to 30m high. Amongst the unique features of the Ardmore tower are its three decorative projecting stringcourses, which divide the tower into four distinct sections.

Round towers were primarily constructed as belfries for churches with a secondary function as storage areas for valuables and places of refuge. They also acted as status symbols and the tower and cathedral testify to the wealth and importance of the twelfth-century Ardmore Monastery. The Romanesque entrance of the tower is located about 4m above ground level, indicative of a refuge function of the tower. The second, third and fourth storeys have small windows and the sixth or bell tower has four windows. The cap has steeper sides than any other Irish tower and is topped by a nineteenth-century cross. Internally there are numerous sculpted corbels with human and animal heads and floral decorations, another unique feature of the Ardmore Tower.

The now-ruined Ardmore Cathedral was built over a number of phases. Its most notable remaining feature is the figure sculpture on the west wall which, according to Tadhg O'Keeffe, 'can probably be attributed to contact with the west of France'. The arcading consists of a row of thirteen panels of which nine still contain Romanesque sculptures. Below these are two semi-circular frames or lunettes that also contain sculptures. Some of the iconography is easily identified. The largest of the thirteen panels clearly shows the figure of Christ with his right hand raised in blessing with the Archangel Michael and a kneeling chalice bearer to his left. 'The Weighing of Souls' features on another with the Devil trying to unbalance the ratio of lost to saved souls. The first lunette of the lower panels features Adam and Eve and an equestrian figure. 'The Judgement of Solomon' with David the harpist in attendance and 'The Adoration of the Magi' are illustrated on the second panel. The side walls of the nave have unusual Romanesque blind arcading.

Two other buildings on the site are of the early Christian period. St Declan's Chapel (Temple Dysart), which was reroofed in 1716, is a small rectangular structure with a long cavity in the floor, which is reputedly the burial place of St Declan. The site also contains a small church whose sides are preserved in the chancel of the cathedral and constitute the first phase of its construction.

REGINALD'S TOWER

Reginald's Tower is one of the great iconic buildings of Waterford city and one of the six towers that form the finest surviving example of medieval defences in Ireland. It is considered to be Ireland's oldest civic building, has been in continuous use for almost 900 years and is the only urban building in Ireland to retain its original Norse name.

The tower derives its name from the Hiberno-Viking leader Ragnall Mac Gillemaire who was imprisoned there in 1170 by the invading English forces led by Strongbow. A tower was first built on the site by the Vikings after 914 and formed the apex of the triangular-shaped Viking settlement. It was rebuilt by the Anglo-Normans in the twelfth century; the ground and first floor levels were most likely constructed during the reign of King John (1199–1216) and were made of shale. The second and third floors were constructed of limestone rubble in the fifteenth and sixteenth centuries. The tower's spiral staircase was orientated to the right, which made it impossible for right-handed attackers to swing their swords properly as they climbed the stairs, and contained 'stumble steps' of different heights and widths to make it difficult for attackers to climb.

Reginald's Tower has been a multi-functional building over the centuries. Both King John and King Edward I minted coins in the city, most likely in Reginald's Tower, and in 1463 the Irish Parliament decreed that a mint be established there. It was also used as an arsenal, especially during Perkin Warbeck's siege in July 1495. In 1819, the tower was converted into 'a place of correction for vagrants and sturdy beggars' and by 1861 it was the home of the city's high constable. In 1954, Reginald's Tower became a museum and opened to the public for the first time.

LISMORE CASTLE: A CAVENDISH HOME IN IRELAND

Lismore Castle acted as the Bishop's Palace until 1589, when Miler McGrath, the then Bishop of Waterford and Lismore, first leased and later sold the castle and lands to Sir Walter Raleigh, who was rarely in residence and spent little time in the town. Richard Boyle, the man who became the 1st Earl of Cork and a great land speculator, purchased the Raleigh estate of 42,000 acres for £1,500 and rebuilt the castle and town. Boyle, according to legend, arrived in Ireland in 1588 with £27 in his pocket, a diamond ring and a bracelet and at the time of his death was one of the richest and most powerful men in Ireland.

In 1610, Richard Boyle began reconstructing the Bishop's Palace as his home. The Gate House, the fortified garden walls and the Riding

House have survived from this time. The town and castle were sacked in 1645; some restoration was carried out by the 2nd Earl of Cork (1612–1694) but from then until 1800 the castle was neglected.

The Cavendish line came to Lismore in 1748 when Charlotte Boyle married William Cavendish, the future 4th Duke of Devonshire. When their grandson, William George Spencer Cavendish, became the 6th duke in 1811, he inherited an immense property portfolio that included Lismore Castle. The 'Bachelor Duke' was a man with a great love for estate improvement and Lismore Castle became one of his pet projects. He first visited Lismore in 1812 and commissioned the remodelling of the castle by the English architect William Atkinson, a specialist in Gothic architecture. Over the next two years the work of reconstructing the habitable part of the castle was completed at a cost of £23,500, and reroofing and further structural restoration were finished by 1822. When the duke visited that year he attended ploughing matches and entertained neighbours to dinners and balls. According to his biographer, James Lees-Milne, his 'attachment to the people and neighbourhood dated from his visit'.

This ended the duke's first phase of development and nothing more was done until October 1840 when Joseph Paxton was introduced to the wonders of Lismore. Paxton, the head gardener at the duke's Chatsworth estate, was an architect, a pioneer of glasshouse design, a publisher of gardening magazines, the designer of the Crystal Palace for the Great Exhibition in London (1851) and an MP from 1854–65. He remained a loyal servant of the Bachelor Duke until his death in 1858. On his 1840 visit, the duke was inspired to make improvements and, according to Lees-Milne, he was 'undoubtedly encouraged by the extraordinary fervour of Paxton who instantly fell in love with the palace. Paxton at once saw endless scope for his architectural talents as well as great horticultural potential in the soil and climate'.

The duke returned in 1844, inspired by the need to sell properties because his debts had exceeded £1 million. He arrived in Lismore in July 1844 and immediately had misgivings about selling one of his prized assets; thus the sale of Lismore was excluded from the retrenchment packet. Instead, the Duke and Paxton engaged in their great redevelopment work on the castle between 1849 and 1858. Paxton was responsible for the architecture and John Gregory Grace for the decoration. John Brown, the head mason at Chatsworth, was sent to Lismore and, as clerk of works, supervised the day-to-day work. Stone quarried and cut to measurement at Chatsworth was transported by boat to Lismore for the castle windows and doors. Grace's plans for converting the ruined chapel were approved and by September 1850 it was spectacularly recreated as an ecclesiastical-style banqueting hall, complete with choir stalls and huge perpendicular stained-glass windows at either end. The roof timbers were painted in vivid red, blue and gold; the space between the velvet-patterned wallpaper and the roof was stencilled with armorial shields intertwined with foliage and included the Devonshire coat of arms of three stags' heads with the motto '*Cavendo tutus*' ('safe through caution') and their crest, a curled, hissing serpent. The Gothic-style windows were from the firm of John Hardman of Birmingham who also supplied the massive concave chandelier and brass Gothic wall brackets. The chimneypiece, a later installation, came from London's Great Exhibition as did the Minton tiles of blue, red and yellow within the fireplace. In this banqueting hall, the duke staged two entertainments annually, one for the local gentry, and the other for the tenants and tradesmen of Lismore and surrounding areas.

In the early 1850s, the entire castle was remodelled to Paxton's design, with the help of his son-in-law G.H. Stokes. The pointed gables were replaced by flat roofs with battlements and eight towers were renovated and decorated with crenellations, merlons, embrasures, bartizans and arrows. The three remaining sides of the courtyard were rebuilt with impressive battlemented towers and turrets with cut stone shipped from Derbyshire.

Lismore Castle is still used as a Cavendish family residence. The present duke, Peregrine Andrew Morny Cavendish, 12th Duke of Devonshire, succeeded to the title in 2004. In the *Sunday Times* Rich List of 2016 he was ranked at number 131. The newspaper citation stated that 'He owns Lismore Castle and one of Ireland's finest collections of art, furniture and craftwork. Devonshire's art collection is worth £900 million and his 75,000 acres are worth £270 million'.

CURRAGHMORE HOUSE AND DEMESNE

In 1776, Arthur Young wrote that 'Curraghmore is one of the finest places in Ireland or indeed that I have anywhere seen'. The house formed an appropriate residence for one of the most powerful families in Ireland, 'the real rulers of the Irish kingdom' during the period of the Protestant Ascendancy; according to one observer, 'Their influence permeated every government department, their relatives occupied every key position'. The family produced a succession of notable politicians, churchmen and soldiers. Arthur Young's description remains valid and today Curraghmore is home to Lord Waterford, Henry de la Poer, 9th Marquis of Waterford. Over 1,000 hectares of formal gardens, woodland and grazing land make Curraghmore the largest private demesne in Ireland. It is surrounded by a boundary wall that stretches for almost 20km, much of which was built as a Famine-relief project.

In 1654, the Civil Survey recorded, 'a fayre Castle and a goodly stone house upon the land, there is also an Orcharde and a Meadow upon the same and stands by the side of a fine wood, the river Clodeth running within a musket shot thereof on the South upon which there is a bridge not very farr from the said castle'. King John's bridge, the oldest structure in the demesne, was built in 1205 across the River Clodiagh and is the oldest bridge in Ireland. It was reputed to have been built for King John's intended visit to Curraghmore but the monarch changed his mind and did not visit the estate. Amongst the features of the multi-arched bridge are the recesses in the stonewalls which allowed those crossing the bridge to step aside smartly and not impede the progress of the lord.

The original tower was rebuilt in 1700 and was subsequently enlarged and remodelled. It was part of the old le Poer family tower house and now forms the centrepiece of Curraghmore House. James Power, 8th Lord Power and 3rd Earl of Tyrone, inherited the estate in 1693, and added the Mansion House to the tower-house structure. The Beresford family came to Curraghmore in 1717 when Sir Marcus Beresford married James' only daughter, the fifteen-year-old heiress Lady Catherine.

With access to the Beresford wealth, Catherine had a remarkable impact on the development of Curraghmore. The Great Room on the first floor of the old tower was Catherine's work in which the plasterwork is attributed to Paul and Phillip Franchini. The Dutch painter Johann van der Hagen was commissioned to decorate the interior with frescoes; the gardens were elaborately laid out with canals, cascades, terraces and statues, which were removed in the late-eighteenth century when formality became unfashionable. At one stage during the nineteenth century, the garden contained a large cast-iron fountain purchased at the Paris Exhibition for £3,000 by the 4th Marquis, but this was later sold for scrap metal by his son.

The Continental-style forecourt of Curraghmore House is one of its most extraordinary features. Its exact date and architect are uncertain but it is generally accepted to be a mid-eighteenth-century construction, and a creation of the great Waterford city architect, John Roberts. Each forecourt side contains long stable ranges dominated by towering pedimented archways and decorated stonework featuring rusticated arches and window surrounds, pedimented niches with statues and doorways with entablatures. The stabling was capable of accommodating up to sixty horses, an essential requirement for a family that was immersed in hunting and racing.

In 1789, George Beresford, the eldest son of Marcus and Catherine, was created the 1st Marquis of Waterford and he enlarged and remodelled the house in the 1790s. The Staircase Hall was built in the inner court. The English architect James Wyatt was commissioned to redecorate the interior of the house and he has been credited with creating some of the finest eighteenth-century rooms in Ireland at Curraghmore. The Dining Room and the Blue Drawing Room are particularly noteworthy with their delicately plastered walls and ceilings, the work of Antonio Zucchi or his wife Angelica Kaufmann and Peter de Gree. George Beresford was also responsible for building the round tower-type structure known as 'The Steeple' in the north-eastern corner of the demesne as a memorial to his twelve-year-old son who was killed in a horse-riding accident. The tower and the house were refaced in the mid-nineteenth century. The crest of the Le Poer family, consisting of the stag of St Hubert with a crucifix between its antlers, dominates the top of the tower. The Beresford family crest of a dragon's head with its neck pierced by a broken spear and with the broken-off point of the spear in the dragon's mouth is to the front of the house.

Henry, 3rd Marquis of Waterford, was renowned for his brilliance and wildness in equal measure. The exploits of Henry and his friends at Melton Mowbray in 1837 are reputed to have introduced the phrase 'painting the town red' to the English language; he is also said to have ridden his horse upstairs in the Kilkenny Club House Hotel, jumped the dining-room table and ridden back down again.

He apparently repeated the performance at Curraghmore. One of the curiosities in Curraghmore House is a swishing block proudly carrying an inscription explaining that it was stolen from Eton by Henry in 1836.

DROMANA GATE LODGE: ONE OF A KIND

The gate lodge at Dromana Bridge is the only example of a Hindu-Gothic building in Ireland and was constructed for the Villiers Stuart estate at Dromana at the end of the bridge over the Finnisk River. Gate lodges were used to regulate entrance to landed estates and also created an important first impression for visitors. Many gate lodges, therefore, displayed extravagant and exotic entrances.

Henry Villiers Stuart inherited the estate in 1824 and came to national prominence in 1826 when he successfully contested the General Election in Waterford as a Protestant pro-Catholic-emancipation candidate, defeating the sitting MP, Lord George Beresford.

The Hindu-Gothic gate lodge has its origins in the marriage of Henry Villiers Stuart to Pauline Ott in 1826. A temporary archway was built by tenants of the estate to mark the couple's return from their honeymoon. They were so impressed by the gesture that they decided to rebuild the structure in more durable materials as a gate lodge based on a plan designed by the architect Martin Day who worked on Dromana House in the early 1820s. The couple had honeymooned in Brighton, where they had seen the King George IV Royal Pavilion, renowned for its use of Hindu and Chinese architecture. A number of parallels are evident between the two structures. A copper dome is used at the centre over the archway, both have flanking lodges and minarets and both serve the same function as entry points. However, the most important comparison can be made between the Dromana lodge and Brighton's North Gate, which was not built until 1832, after the death of King George and after the Villiers Stuart marriage. Historian Trisha Ryan suggests that when the time came to construct the permanent structure, either the architect or the couple revisited Brighton and may have used the newly constructed North Gate as a template for the gate lodge at Dromana.

Although it had a number of practical purposes, the Dromana lodge was clearly built to demonstrate the wealth and prestige of the Dromana estate. The extension of the structure into a bridge allowed the visitor to view the lodge as a whole from afar and added to the sense of arrival into a great estate. As the lodge had the same design from both sides, the visitor was again reminded of its splendour on leaving the estate.

The single-storey Hindu-Gothic gate lodge is an example of a twin lodge with a single-celled room on each side of a road, with an archway joining the two. The gatekeeper's family dined on one side and the other side acted as a common room used for rest and sleep. The redbrick ceilings are vaulted and the external roofs are flat, hidden by parapets of Gothic trefoil design. The archway was wide enough to allow a carriage to enter and exit. The combination of the arch and the lodge form a triumphal archway.

The copper-clad ogee-shaped onion dome, located over the central point of the archway, is the most obvious Hindu-inspired design feature. The dome sits on top of an octagonal stone structure that is hidden behind the parapet, and this creates the impression that the dome is emerging from the top of the parapet. The upper part of the dome is finished with a Hindu-style minaret; eight minarets were also used in the construction and are placed at the top of decorative corner posts.

The lodge fell into disrepair during the 1900s and by the 1960s was in an advanced state of decay. The intervention of the Georgian Society and local fundraising efforts were instrumental in restoring the structure. Further repairs were made by the Waterford County Council in 1990.

THE FOLLY OF BALLYSAGGARTMORE TOWERS

Situated close to Lismore but unconnected to the castle is the extraordinary folly of the Ballysaggartmore Towers, constructed by the discredited landlord Arthur Kiely-Ussher in the 1830s. Kiely inherited an estate of 8,000 acres in 1808 and changed his name to the more upmarket Kiely-Ussher to more appropriately honour his new standing. His mansion, Ballysaggartmore House, included two drawing rooms, an imposing dining room, a conservatory, a billiard room and a study and morning room at ground-floor level.

Eleven bedrooms, a nursery room, a schoolroom and bathrooms were located on the upper floor. This was not enough, however. Kiely-Ussher's wife, Elizabeth, conscious of her status in society and extremely jealous of her brother-in-law John Kiely, who resided in the imposing Strancally Castle overlooking the River Blackwater, urged her husband to construct a similar mansion.

The Ballysaggartmore Towers were built to mark the entrance of what was planned to be the new Kiely-Ussher mansion. The entrance gate consisted of a pointed arch flanked by miniature Gothic castles, intended as gatekeepers' lodges. The Inner Gates are even more grandiose and include two sets of towers and turrets that guard both ends of a bridge over a sculpted stream. In 1834 the *Dublin Penny Journal* claimed the towers embraced 'almost every shape and style of Gothic architecture'. A third, less spectacular, servants' tunnel was also built. Local stone was used and the overall cost of the project amounted to £2,000 with another £150 invested in manufacturing iron gates. The intervention of the Great Famine ended Kiely-Ussher's grandiose plans and he earned a notorious reputation for his policy of evicting tenants during the famine. John Keeffe tried to assassinate Kiely-Ussher but his gun jammed and his target escaped unhurt; Keeffe and his six co-conspirators were arrested, tried and transported to Van Diemen's Land in October 1849. The Kiely-Ussher estate fell into bankruptcy in the early 1850s and the entire house and lands were offered for sale under the Encumbered Estates Act and eventually sold in 1861. Ballysaggartmore House was burnt during the Civil War and the ruin was demolished after the Second World War.

CURRAGHMORE SHELL HOUSE

Ireland in the 1740s experienced something of a mania for the building of grottoes. The Shell House, built in Curraghmore by Lady Catherine, is of this tradition. When Charles Smith wrote his history in 1746 it was still at the construction stage but he stated that 'when finished [it] promises to be very curious'. The grotto's interior was encrusted with shells of every shape, colour and magnitude and in the centre John van Nost's marble statue of the countess recognises Catherine's contribution to its construction.

In one hand she holds a shell and in the other a scroll stating that 'In two hundred and sixty one days these shells were put up by the proper hands of the Rtr. Honorabel Cathne Countess of Tyrone'.

MOUNT CONGREVE GARDENS: A GREAT GARDEN OF THE WORLD

According to Jane Powers, author of *The Irish Garden,* Ambrose Congreve was 'probably the most avaricious have-it-all plantsman Ireland has ever known and his Waterford garden remains a monument to his massive appetite for plants.' Over a period of eight decades, Congreve filled his garden with thousands of plants. Congreve was born in 1907 at 3 Savile Row, London, the building which later provided a rooftop stage for the Beatles' final concert. He died in 2011 aged 104. Mount Congreve House is located about 5 miles from Waterford city and was constructed in the 1760s for John Congreve, Ambrose's great-great-great grandfather. Ambrose Congreve divided his time between Mount Congreve and a large house in the St James's area of London, where he entertained lavishly.

Ambrose Congreve was fortunate; as a teenager he met his extraordinary horticultural mentor, the banker Lionel de Rothschild. In 1919, de Rothschild purchased the Mitford estate at Exbury in Hampshire, where he created one of the finest gardens in England with more than one million plants. He also co-sponsored global plant-hunting expeditions to collect seed for plant growth and experimentation. Ambrose Congreve's childhood visits to Exbury ignited his love of gardening and it was de Rothschild's taste and style that provided the inspiration for the later plantings at Mount Congreve.

Lionel de Rothschild provided Congreve with an endless supply of plants that were sent, carriage paid, to Waterford. Ambrose Congreve began the serious work of creating his Mount Congreve Gardens in the mid-1950s when almost 70 acres of 'robber trees' were cleared. In 1961 Dutch expert Herman Dool was appointed gardening director at Mount Congreve and he was a key influence on the development. Mass planting characterised Ambrose Congreve's style at a time when such a luxury was available to only the very wealthy or the well connected. The garden contains over

2,000 varieties of rhododendron, 600 varieties of camellia, over 300 different Japanese maples and over 100 magnolias. It is estimated that the garden includes at least 9,500 different plants. The overall impact is to produce a garden that is, in the words of Joan Powers, 'like a horticultural Vatican, overwhelmingly furnished with showy specimens.' These plantings are overlooked by eighteenth- and nineteenth-century shelter-providing plantations of oak and beech and there are more than 16 miles of paths winding in and around them, now and again, affording fine views of the River Suir.

Lionel de Rothschild's idea that different areas of a garden should shine during different seasons is also exemplified in Mount Congreve, especially in the 4-acre walled garden with its 1960s lake shaped like the Ascot racecourse. The walled garden originated in the eighteenth century and had a practical and aesthetic function. The borders are arranged into May, June, July and August borders, each filled with varieties of herbaceous plants, including special iris beds and hydrangeas. The garden also includes a brightly coloured Chinese pagoda, an artificial waterfall, a wildflower meadow, a bluebell walk and a bamboo garden.

In the post-Second World War years, the Mount Congreve Gardens team successfully competed at the Chelsea Flower Show and won thirteen gold medals for the eighteen gardens exhibited. Congreve was awarded a CBE in 1965 for his services to horticulture, in 1987 he was awarded a Veitch Memorial Medal by the Royal Horticultural Society, and in 2001 a gold medal from the Massachusetts Horticultural Society that recognised Mount Congreve as a Great Garden of the World. Ambrose Congreve was buried with his wife Margaret beneath the Temple in his extraordinary garden.

LISMORE CASTLE GARDENS

Lismore Castle gardens are considered to be the oldest continuously worked gardens in Ireland and cover 7 acres contained within the original seventeenth-century castle walls. They divide into two very different sections. The Upper Garden is a complete example of a seventeenth-century walled garden; the walls and terraces remain as they were when commissioned by Richard Boyle in the early 1600s, although the planting arrangements have changed. It consists of herbaceous borders and a working kitchen garden that supplies fruit, vegetables and herbs for the castle kitchen. The Lower Garden was mainly the creation of the 6th duke and his ace gardener Joseph Paxton. This garden is informal with shrubs, trees and lawns. Camellias, magnolias, rhododendrons and flowering herbaceous borders provide rotational splashes of colour as the seasons evolve. The garden includes species that are native of China, Japan, Chile, New Zealand, the Caucus and Himalayas as well as Great Britain and Ireland, and includes novelties such as the snakebark maple, the Japanese snowbell and the Empress tree. The Yew Avenue is a much older creation that may date to the seventeenth century and is where Edmund Spenser is reputed to have written part of his great poem 'The Faerie Queen'. In recent times a number of contemporary sculptures have been added to the garden, including pieces by Richard Wright, Eilis O'Connell, Franz West and Roger Hiorns. Two sections of the Berlin Wall were installed in the Lower Garden in 2015.

MAHON RAILWAY VIADUCT

The development of the railway in Ireland had a dramatic impact on the landscape. Cuttings, embankments, viaducts and stations were constructed to cater for the new form of transport. Nowhere was this more visible than at Kilmacthomas.

The entry to Kilmacthomas from Carrick-on-Suir is dominated by the magnificent eight-arch stone viaduct built in 1873 by the Waterford, Dungarvan and Lismore Railway Company, which later became part of the Great Southern and Western Railway group. The bridge was designed by James Otway and constructed by the Glaswegian firm of Smith Finlayson & Co. It spans a road, a millrace and the River Mahon. The bridge provides an excellent example of the technical, engineering and masonry expertise required in railway construction. Railway services on the Waterford–Dungarvan line ended in 1982 but the bridge was recently reopened as part of the Waterford–Dungarvan Greenway. Two additional major construction projects associated with the Lismore–Waterford line were the Ballyvoyle Railway Viaduct, which was damaged during the Civil War and rebuilt in 1923, and the Ballyvoyle Tunnel (1878).

6

WATERFORD NOTABLES

Several natives of Waterford apart from those already mentioned have made a significant contribution in their fields of endeavour on the international and domestic fronts. This chapter examines the careers of eight of these individuals.

MARGARET AYLWARD (1810–1889)

Margaret Aylward, a member of one of the most prominent and wealthiest of Waterford's Catholic merchant families, was born on 23 November 1810. She inherited the entrepreneurial gene and became an excellent businesswoman. Her first association with the world of work came as a volunteer lay teacher in the Presentation Sisters' schools, educating the poor girls of the city. Aylward made two attempts to pursue a religious vocation: in 1834 she joined the Irish Sisters of Charity in Dublin but left after a short time; a brief spell as an Ursuline sister in January 1846 also ended in failure.

Margaret moved to Dublin where she quickly established a reputation as one of Dublin's leading charity workers, operating on behalf of the Ladies' Association of the Charity of St Vincent de Paul, especially in the parishes of St Mary's and St Michan's where she established a branch of the association in May 1851. The provision of support was leavened with an emphasis on the importance of maintaining the Catholic faith. Those receiving aid were encouraged to 'frequent the Sacraments, to hear mass on Sundays and Holydays, to urge upon the parents the necessity of making their children attend the catechism'. The neglect of religious practice, Margaret believed, was 'the very cancer of society, the feeder of the poor-house, the prison and the hospital'. In 1853 a practical intervention was taken to provide poor women with training and employment. The St Mary's Industrial Institute was opened in an abandoned coach factory at 5 Upper Dorset Street, Dublin, offering training and employment in basic needlework and embroidery. Sadly, the low-value nature of the work proved to be economically unviable and the institute closed after two years.

The plight of orphaned Catholic children was a particular concern of Margaret; she believed that the traditional orphanage was unsuitable for the rearing of children and that a family environment was essential. The St Brigid's Orphanage was opened on 1 January 1857. The main purpose of St Brigid's was to find long-term foster homes for orphaned children, preferably in a rural environment in the surrounding counties where 'there is the least amount of vice and the least amount of danger of contamination'. During the period 1868–74, the orphanage had an average of 292 children in its care at any one time. Children placed with farm families were expected to be given age-appropriate work on the land – this did not always happen, despite the twice-yearly inspections. Margaret developed one of the largest and most complex child-care organisations in the country, which defied practically every contemporary movement, and by the time of her death she had undertaken the long-term care of 2,717 children. It was a pioneering venture that lead to her imprisonment.

In April 1858 Margaret was imprisoned for failure to comply with a writ of *habeas corpus* and was sentenced to six months' imprisonment in Grangegorman on a charge of contempt of court. She emerged from prison with a new mission in life to pursue the education of the 'more abandoned, more destitute children' of the city. She opened her first Catholic School of St Brigid in Cow Street in Dublin's Temple Bar district on 7 October 1860. By 1870 five schools had been established with the centrality of religious instruction their principal distinguishing feature.

Margaret Aylward had time for one more initiative. She founded the Sisters of the Holy Faith in 1864. Religious names and dress were adopted but entrance dowries were not required, which, along with the elimination of differentiation between lay and choir sisters, distinguished the new congregation, defying conventional wisdom and bringing religious life within the reach of poorer women. In 1865

Glasnevin House and grounds were purchased as a motherhouse by Margaret and in 1866 Archbishop Paul Cullen formally granted congregational status to the order. Margaret maintained an independent lifestyle and steered well clear of a cloistered existence, though in her later years illness prevented her from travelling. Margaret died on 11 October 1889 and was buried in the convent cemetery.

ROBERT BOYLE (1627–1691)

Robert Boyle, 'the father of modern chemistry', was born in Lismore Castle on 27 January 1627, the youngest and favourite son of the Great Earl of Cork, Richard Boyle and his second wife Catherine Fenton. Robert spent his early childhood at Lismore where he was fostered to a local family and learned to speak Irish before he was sent to Eton, at the age of 8. At 11, he was taken out of school and tutored at the earl's new English base, Stalbridge House, and shortly after departed on a Grand Tour of Europe with his older brother Francis. Robert returned to England in 1644 and devoted his life to writing and scientific research. He was responsible for one of the most significant breakthroughs in the history of science – Boyle's Law, which describes the relationship between the pressure and volume of a gas at a constant temperature. Boyle's discovery made possible the creation of many devices, such as pressure cookers, aerosols, syringes, soft-drink cans, engines and compression tools. The use of steam power provided the foundation of the industrial revolution.

Boyle practised as a scientist at a time when the discipline was heavy on theory and light on experimentation and his emphasis on experimentation was critical in the development of modern science and scientific practice. He published his findings in a form that encouraged other scientists to repeat his experiments, thus initiating the process of the sharing and the retesting of results and experiments. He also co-founded the Royal Society in London in the 1660s, an organisation founded to promote and support excellence in science and to place experimentation at its centre.

In 1661, Boyle published *The Sceptical Chymist*, which secured his reputation as the Father of Modern Chemistry and challenged the still popular Aristotelian view that the four elements of earth, air, water and fire formed the ingredients of all things.

Boyle was also deeply interested in philosophy and theology. As a director of the East India Company, he spent large sums promoting the spread of Christianity. Boyle firmly believed that the Bible should be available in the vernacular and in the 1680s he bankrolled the printing of both the Old and New Testaments in the Irish language. In this respect, Boyle's attitude to the Irish language differed from others of his class, who largely opposed its use both as a language of worship and as a means of communication.

THOMAS FRANCIS MEAGHER (1823–1867)

Thomas Francis Meagher was born in Waterford on 3 August 1823, the eldest child of Thomas and Mary Meagher (*née* Quan) who died four years later. His father played a prominent role in Daniel O'Connell's successful campaign for Catholic Emancipation and became the first Catholic Lord Mayor of Waterford city following the repeal of the anti-Catholic restrictions. He was also elected an MP for the city, serving from 1847 until 1857. The parliamentary route was not for his maverick son Thomas Francis.

The Meagher family were wealthy and Thomas received the best education that Catholic money could buy, attending Clongowes Wood and Stonyhurst, two of the leading Jesuit schools in the United Kingdom. According to legend, he achieved notoriety in Stonyhurst when, as first clarinettist in the school band, he refused to play at the annual celebration of the Battle of Waterloo, a nationalistic act of defiance that forced the musical celebration to be abandoned. At Stonyhurst he enrolled in the School of Rhetoric and dominated the debating society, developing the oratorical skills that were so important in his later life.

Meagher returned to Waterford in 1843 and followed the family tradition by supporting Daniel O'Connell's repeal movement. This was a time of growing divisions between O'Connell and the younger members of the association led by Thomas Davis and others. These Young Irelanders became increasingly disillusioned with O'Connell's non-violent approach and, at a conference of the Repeal Association held at the Conciliation Hall in Dublin on 28 July 1846, Meagher delivered one of his most famous speeches as he justified the use of physical force in pursuit of political independence. Meagher of the Sword was born on this occasion:

> There are times when arms alone will suffice, and when political amelioration call for a drop of blood, and many thousands drops of blood ... force must be used against force. The soldier is proof against an argument, but he is not proof against a bullet ... it is the weaponed arm of the patriot that can alone prevail against battalioned despotism. Then, my lord, I do not disclaim the use of arms as immoral, not do I believe it the truth to say, that the God of heaven withholds his sanction from the use of arms ... Be it for the defence, or be it for the assertion of a nation's liberty, I look upon the sword as a sacred weapon ...

Interrupted in rhetorical mid-flight by John O'Connell and prevented from resuming, Meagher departed the meeting with his fellow leaders of Young Ireland and a new era in Irish politics was initiated.

The split in the movement ultimately led to the 1848 rebellion. In January 1847, the Young Irelanders met in the Rotunda in Dublin and established the Irish Confederation to further the objectives of the Repeal Association. The French Revolution of 1848 provided inspiration and in April, William Smith O'Brien and Meagher travelled to Paris to present the congratulations of the Irish people to the revolutionaries and possibly to elicit support for the Irish cause. Meagher returned from Paris inspired with an idea for a flag for a new Ireland. The tricolour, which eventually became the flag of Ireland, was flown for the first time from the window of the Wolfe Tone Confederation Club at 33 The Mall in Waterford on 7 March 1848. It flew defiantly in Waterford for eight days before it was removed by the authorities. After returning from

France, Meagher brought the flag to Dublin and, at a meeting of the Confederation Club, he explained the significance of the colours.

> The white in the centre signifies a lasting truce between Orange and Green. I trust that beneath its folds the hands of the Irish Catholic and the Irish Protestant may be clasped in generous and heroic brotherhood.

Less than five months later the failed Young Ireland rebellion took place on 28 July 1848 at Ballingarry County Tipperary. In the months prior to the rebellion Meagher's oratorical skills were a prized asset of the Young Irelanders: on 16 July 1848, he addressed a crowd of 50,000 from the summit of Slievenamon and told the assembled that he stood 'upon the lofty summit of a country which, if we do not win for ourselves we must win for those who come after us'. After the rebellion, Meagher was arrested, tried, found guilty of high treason in October 1848 and sentenced to be hung, drawn and quartered.

The sentence was commuted to transportation to Van Diemen's Land, Britain's most distant penal colony. Meagher spent from October 1849 to January 1852 on the island before escaping, abandoning his wife, Catherine, in the process.

Meagher's arrival in New York was sensational. The city's population of 800,000 included 200,000 Irish-born immigrants, most of whom bitterly resented their forced emigration. Meagher was anointed with celebrity status and began a lucrative lecture tour, starting in November in New York, where 6,000 people reportedly attended. He also established the *Irish News* newspaper, which adopted a strong pro-Democratic and pro-Southern stance.

A brief reunion with Catherine failed and Meagher found new love in New York, marrying Elizabeth Townsend, the daughter of a wealthy New York industrialist, on 14 November 1855. He spent much of the late 1850s in Costa Rica and Nicaragua, unsuccessfully promoting the value of building a railway line to link the eastern seaboard with the Pacific Ocean.

Meagher returned to New York in January 1861 as the USA was lurching towards civil war. He was a late convert to the Union cause and as a committed Democrat he supported the party line of non-interference with slavery. The war meant opportunity and advancement and in 1861 Meagher was in dire need of both. After cheating death leading a group of Irish volunteers at the Battle of Bull Run, he returned to New York in July 1861 and spent the month of August recruiting for a new Irish brigade where his status amongst the Irish in America and oratorical skills were seen at their best. The Irish Brigade was founded in late 1861 and Meagher was appointed brigadier general. The brigade had its first military engagement at Fair Oaks in June 1862 and was also heavily engaged in the Seven Days Battles, suffering many casualties. It was during this week of savagery that the Irish Brigade established its reputation for extraordinary courage.

However, Meagher's reputation began to suffer. Stories spread about his tardiness as a camp commander and inefficiency as a field commander, hardly a surprise given his lack of military experience. It was also suggested that his desire for personal acclaim and advancement led him to expose his men recklessly and, as the war progressed, charges of drunkenness and incompetence dogged him.

Meagher lead his troops in more episodes of butchery at the Battle of Antietam and at Fredericksburg, where the Irish Brigade's casualty rate was again enormous. Meagher led the brigade into battle for the last time at Chancellorsville in the spring of 1863. The losses there were the final tipping point for Meagher and he resigned in May 1863.

He regretted the decision almost immediately but his offers to raise another Irish brigade were ignored. He was eventually posted to Nashville, Tennessee, where he was placed in charge of two convalescent brigades of men recovering from injury or illness. When the logistics of moving the division to join with General Sherman at New Bern, North Carolina were mismanaged, Meagher's military career came to an inglorious conclusion. He was relieved of his duties by General Ulysses S. Grant and sent back to New York. He resigned his commission on 15 May 1865.

In 1864 Meagher supported Abraham Lincoln in his re-election campaign. Although this damaged his reputation among the Irish Americans, the majority of whom were against the Republican administration, it enabled the Waterford man to accumulate political capital in the corridors of power in Washington. President Andrew Johnson, who succeeded the assassinated Lincoln, appointed him secretary of the newly created Montana Territory in July 1865 and he also inherited the position of acting governor.

The political situation in Montana at this time was volatile and dominated by poisonous battles between a Republican-inspired minority and the Democratic majority. Prior to Meagher's arrival mine owners, ranchers and the representatives of big business banded together to form vigilante groups to impose law and order, especially in the mining camps. The Native Americans also posed difficulties for Meagher. Members of the Blackfoot tribe had reluctantly ceded thousands of square miles of their land. Groups of Blackfoot warriors refused to accept the forced settlement and launched attacks on individual settlers and miners. To deal with the situation Meagher raised a volunteer militia of 600 soldiers and was promised a consignment of weapons by General Sherman. On 1 July 1867 he arrived at Fort Benton to take delivery of the weapons. He was offered accommodation aboard the *G. A. Thompson* by its Irish captain, John Doran. It was here that he disappeared over night. His body was never recovered.

Several theories were put forward to explain his death. His enemies suggested that Meagher had staggered along the upper deck in a drunken stupor and fallen overboard. His supporters suggested that illness had caused him to stagger overboard. A broken handrail on the upper deck, temporarily repaired by a section of rope, may have contributed to a tragic accident. The Democrats favoured the idea that Meagher was assassinated by hitmen sent by Montana vigilantes; the Irish-American constituency preferred the theory that he was murdered by agents of the British Government. The Fenian Brotherhood was also touted as a remote possibility, as Meagher had opposed a planned invasion of Canada from the USA.

His contribution to Irish and American history is recognised in statues of Meagher on horseback at The Mall in Waterford city and in Helena, capital city of Montana. A monument at the Antietam battlefield was dedicated in his honour and is inscribed with a brief biographical outline of Meagher's career. In March 2015, the Suir Bridge, which crosses the River Suir outside Waterford, was renamed the Thomas Francis Meagher Bridge.

DERVLA MURPHY (b.1931)

Dervla Murphy is one of Ireland's finest travel writers. The extent of her travels, her sociological and political insight and the breadth of her learning are truly extraordinary and have resulted in twenty-six published books. In 1979 Murphy published her biography, *Wheels within Wheels,* which, according to *The Times*, is 'An extraordinary book, reflecting an extraordinary woman and one of the great travellers of our time'.

Murphy was born in Waterford on 28 November 1931 and was educated at the Ursuline Convent. When she was fourteen she was forced to leave in order to nurse her mother who suffered from severe arthritis. This work continued for sixteen years, interspersed with occasional cycling breaks in Europe. Her mother's death released her from her domestic responsibilities and in 1963 she cycled across Europe to India. Her two-year sojourn included time spent working with Tibetan refugee children. On her return to Lismore she published her first book, *Full Tilt: Ireland to India with a Bicycle,* in 1965, followed by *Tibetan Foothold*. In 1966, Dervla made her first trip to Africa; this time her chosen mode of travel was by pack mule and the journey proved to be the inspiration behind *In Ethiopia with a Mule*. In 1968, Dervla's only child, Rachel, was born. As a single parent, Murphy continued her travels and, at five years of age, Rachel accompanied Dervla on a trip to India; they flew into Bombay and travelled to Goa and Coorg. This trip was documented in *On a Shoestring to Coorg*. The pair later journeyed to Baltistan, recounted in *Where the Indus is Young*, Peru (*Eight Feet in the Andes*), Madagascar (*Muddling through in Madagascar*) and the Cameroons (*Cameroon with Egbert*).

In the autumn of 2005, she visited Cuba with Rachel and three granddaughters Rose, Clodagh and Zea, all under ten years of age, who were considered by Dervla to be 'old enough to benefit from some real travelling, instead of merely flying from their home in Italy to visit relatives and friends in Wales, England and Ireland'. This trip and two return trips made in 2006 and 2007 were described in *The Island that Dared* (2008).

In the late 1970s, Dervla's work adopted a sharper political edge, beginning with the publication of *A Place Apart* (1978), based on her travels and insight gained from her short-term residency in Northern Ireland with both sides of the community divide. This work won the Christopher Ewart-Briggs Memorial Prize in 1979. The publication in 1982 of *Race to the Finish? The Nuclear Stakes* continued this trend, as did other works that explored racial relationships in Birmingham and Bradford, the impact of AIDS on Kenya and Zimbabwe, post-apartheid life in South Africa, genocide in Rwanda, tribal displacement in Laos and post-war reconstruction in Balkan Europe.

In 2002, a serious knee injury disrupted her plans to cycle through eastern Russia; instead of cycling, she embarked on a journey through Siberia by train, boat and bus, which she documented in *Through Siberia by Accident* (2005). She revisited Siberia and wrote a companion book, *Silverland: A Journey Beyond the Urals* (2006).

Dervla has focused on another of the world's trouble spots for her latest works: in the summer of 2011, she spent a month in the Gaza Strip and described her stay in *A Month by the Sea* (2013); in 2015, she wrote about further encounters with Israelis and Palestinians in *Between River and Sea: Encounters in Israel and Palestine*.

EDMUND RICE (1762–1844)

In 1779, Edmund Rice, a native of Callan, County Kilkenny, began an apprenticeship in Waterford in the business of his uncle Michael, a successful merchant. Edmund quickly established a reputation as a skilled entrepreneur and for his religious devotion (he was known to recite the rosary as he travelled to the markets). In 1785, he married Mary Elliott, a tanner's daughter who tragically died in January 1789, leaving Edmund a twenty-seven-year-old widower and the father of a special-needs daughter.

The death of Mary was a defining moment in Edmund's spiritual evolution. He formed a confraternity with a number of like-minded young Waterford men with a commitment to lead more active Christian lives. They promoted the practice of charity and, unusually for the time, the frequent reception of the sacraments.

The Presentation Sisters opened a school in Waterford in 1798 with a mission to educate poor Catholic girls. Edmund, by now a wealthy man, generously supported them and acted as their business manager and agent. He also began a mission to replicate

Nano Nagle's system for the poor Catholic boys of Waterford city, starting teaching in an old stable in New Street, where three rooms were fitted out as a school in 1802. Benches were borrowed each day from an alehouse in Barrack Street. Teachers and pupils learned together and a second school was opened in nearby Stephen Street. In June 1803, Bishop Hussey officially opened their new residence at Ballybricken, which became the internationally famous Mount Sion. Hussey died the same year and his successor and Rice's longtime associate John Power blessed and opened the Mount Sion School on 1 May 1804 with 300 enrolled pupils. A night school was opened to cater for the illiterate masses and provide them with religious instruction. A bakery was also operated to provide the poorest students with a basic bread-and-milk diet and a tailor was employed to repair ragged clothes and distribute suits to the poor.

By 1810 Edmund Rice had his tightly regimented, minutely planned system of education in place. Students were grouped 'according to their rate of improvement' rather than their age; the teaching brothers were supported by monitors and their combined efforts catered for classes of up to 150 boys; a well-stocked lending library operated in the school and the boys were encouraged to read the books with their parents at night. Considerable time was devoted to moral instruction, with times set for prayer and catechism lessons considered to be 'the most salutary part of the system'.

Edmund Rice's system of education expanded rapidly. His contacts inspired wealthy Catholics to finance similar ventures and schools were opened in Carrick-on-Suir, Thurles and Limerick (1806), Dungarvan (1807), Cork (1811) and in 1818 Cork's famous North Monastery opened its doors. Edmund Rice also sent communities to cater for the poor of the industrial cities of England beginning in Preston (1825) and Manchester and, in 1826, in Soho in London.

Edmund Rice and his companions lived the life of a religious community. The members of what eventually became the Irish Christian Brothers assembled annually at Mount Sion and took vows according to the rule and constitution of the Presentation Order. In 1820, the community received approval from Pope Pius VII and, over the next decade, the members adapted the rules of the Jesuits, the De La Salle brothers and the Presentation sisters to suit their own needs. Finally, in 1832, the rule of the Irish Christian Brothers was printed.

Edmund Rice retired as superior general of the Irish Christian Brothers in 1838, after thirty-six years of leadership. He died on 29 August 1844. At the time of his death, the Irish Christian Brothers ran forty-three schools, including six in England.

LUKE WADDING (1588–1657)

Few Waterford individuals have assembled a portfolio of achievement to match that of Luke Wadding, the son of a wealthy Waterford merchant who was born in the city in 1588 and received his initial education there. After the death of his parents, he entered the Irish College at Lisbon as a seminarian but left the college, joined the Franciscans and was ordained a priest in 1613. Mentored by Antonio de Trejo, the vicar-general of the Franciscan Order, he was appointed professor of theology at Salamanca. In 1618, de Trejo was appointed by Philip III of Spain to travel to Rome on a mission to persuade the pope to recognise the Immaculate Conception of the Blessed Virgin Mary as a dogma of Catholic faith. Wadding was appointed theologian of the delegation.

The mission, though unsuccessful, brought new opportunities to Wadding, who remained in Rome for the rest of his life. Popes Paul V (1602–21), Gregory XV (1621–23), cardinals and curia officials were all impressed by Wadding's qualities. In 1625, Wadding accepted responsibility for the unfinished and debt-ridden St Isidore's church in Rome, on condition that he be allowed establish a college there for the training of Franciscan priests for Ireland. Wadding cleared the debts, completed the construction work and hired many distinguished artists to work at St Isidore's. The college became a first-class school of philosophy and theology and supplied numerous Franciscan preachers and missionaries to Ireland and elsewhere. Under Wadding's influence Irish Franciscan colleges were established in Prague, Vielun (Poland), Paris and Capranica (Italy). Between 1625 and 1660 St Isidore's supplied over seventy professors of philosophy and theology to Franciscan and other colleges across the continent. Wadding also founded a small seminary for Irish secular priests in Rome that was eventually to become the Pontifical Irish College in Rome and a third college (founded 1856) for the training of Irish novices, approximately 60km north of Rome.

In 1623 Wadding published the first printed edition of the writings of St Francis. This began a publishing career that averaged a volume annually until his death in 1657. Despite suffering from ill health, Wadding published many diverse works, including biographies of St Thomas of Aquitaine and St Anselm of Lucia, a volume on the death of the Virgin Mary and an edited edition of the works of Duns Scotus in 1639, which revived interests in the philosophies of the medieval Franciscan.

As a Vatican insider and respected by the leading curia figures of the day, Wadding was influential politically. On his appointment to the Congregation of the Breviary in Rome he included St Patrick's Day among the official saints' days for the first time. Following the disturbances of 1641 he was a powerful supporter of the Confederate Catholics who appointed Wadding as their accredited agent in Rome with instructions to obtain papal sanction and finance. Urban VIII had no interest in supporting the Irish cause but Wadding was more successful with his successor, Innocent X. Through Wadding's efforts Archbishop Rinnucini was appointed nuncio to Ireland. He also engineered the return to Ireland of Owen Roe O'Neill, the greatest Irish general of the time.

Wadding died on 18 November 1657 and was buried at St Isidore's College in Rome, the college he had inherited and rescued from financial ruin in 1625.

ERNEST WALTON (1903–1995)

Another scientist with Waterford connections is Ernest Walton, although his connection to the county is rather tenuous. He was born in Abbeyside on 6 October 1903, the son of Revd John Arthur Walton from Cloughjordan, County Tipperary and Anna Elizabeth Sinton from Richill, County Armagh. John Arthur Walton was a Methodist minister who lived the peripatetic lifestyle that was typical of the religion's ministers of the time. The family were based in Abbeyside for the first three years of Ernest's life, before transferring to Rathkeale, County Limerick and then to Ulster, where most of his education took place. He received his second-level education at Methodist College, Belfast and, after graduating from Dublin University, he entered Cambridge in 1927 and studied with the great pioneer of nuclear physics, Ernest Rutherford. He was awarded his PhD in 1931.

On 14 April 1932, Ernest Walton succeeded in splitting the nucleus of an atom by artificial means by using a piece of lithium metal and striking it with positively charged particles called protons which smashed the nuclei of some of the lithium atoms into pieces. Rutherford had predicted that when the atomic nucleus was split alpha particles would appear and Walton was the first to see these particles on that fateful April day when the atomic age began. He had succeeded by using far lower electrical voltage than was hitherto believed possible. Overnight, Walton became Ireland's most famous living scientist and retained this distinction until his death in 1995.

In 1951, Walton and his colleague John Cockcroft were awarded the Nobel Prize in Physics for their work. Walton is the only Irish man to receive such an award in a science subject. He returned to Ireland in 1934 as a Fellow of Trinity College where he lectured and researched for the remainder of his career. During the Second World War, he was invited to join the Manhattan Project in the USA, working on the development of the atomic bomb, but was refused leave of absence by the college authorities. In 1989, he was given a civic reception in Dungarvan and the Causeway Park was named in his honour.

THOMAS WYSE (1791–1862)

Thomas Wyse, a member of one of Waterford's most distinguished and oldest Catholic families, was comfortable with his English nationality and a committed defender of the union with Britain. He was born in Waterford on 24 December 1791, was educated in Stonyhurst College and studied law at Trinity College Dublin where he was one of the few Catholic students. His experience convinced him of the value of mixed education and its potential to end the bitter religious divisions in Ireland. In 1815 Thomas Wyse embarked on a decade-long Grand Tour, travelling extensively in south-eastern Europe, North Africa and the Middle East.

The trip included a visit to Lucien Bonaparte, younger brother of the Emperor Napoleon, where he was introduced to Lucien's pretty eleven-year-old daughter, the Princess Letitia. He returned later and on 4 March 1821, the thirty-year-old Thomas Wyse married sixteen-year-old Letitia Bonaparte at Canino in Italy. Their first son, Napoleon Alfred, was born on 6 January 1822.

The marriage was an unhappy one. Apart from a significant age gap, the couple were personally incompatible. Thomas Wyse was a serious and scholarly individual, a polyglot, and a lover of Greek culture who read the New Testament in its original language. Letitia was a socialite who enjoyed a good time. In August 1825 the family returned to Waterford and resided with George Wyse in a house on The Adelphi. The following year their second son, William Charles was born. Letitia soon became disenchanted with life in Waterford and the differences between the couple became more obvious and pronounced. Letitia abandoned Waterford and the marriage in 1828 but returned later in the year to procure a Deed of Separation.

In the General Election of 1826 Henry Villiers-Stuart sensationally defeated the sitting MP Lord George Thomas Beresford, a member of one of the most powerful political dynasties in the United Kingdom who had held the Waterford seat unchallenged since 1806. As part of its campaign to achieve Catholic emancipation, the Catholic Association opposed Beresford in the Waterford constituency. The mastermind of this victory was Wyse, who introduced the novel strategy of canvassing the largely Catholic electorate to vote for Villiers-Stuart and engage in an act of political mutiny by defying their landlords.

The victory ultimately led to Catholic Emancipation in 1829. Wyse was one of those who immediately benefitted from the removal of the political shackles as he was elected MP for County Tipperary in 1830 (the second Catholic elected following the emancipation legislation), and represented his native city from 1835 to 1847.

Wyse's chief parliamentary interest lay in education. He believed that all classes had a right to education, irrespective of religious affiliation, and that the state had a responsibility to finance this education. He developed a plan for a national system of education involving universal elementary schools for all classes, secondary education for the middle classes and university education for the elite of society. In his first term in parliament Wyse lobbied the influential for support for his system of education. In July 1831, he addressed the MPs and told them that 'Education, which in other countries is a blessing, in Ireland ... has become a positive curse ... has all along been a mere matter of religious and political partisanship'. Wyse's interventions had a positive impact and Lord Stanley, the chief secretary of Ireland, implemented Wyse's ideas. A national education board was established to finance a system, paying approximately two-thirds of the building costs, contributing towards the teacher's salary and supplying cheap textbooks to local committees or individuals whose applications were successful. Pupils of all denominations were instructed together in secular subjects with religious instruction delivered separately on one or two days each week by teachers approved by the clergy of the different denominations. The National School system established in 1831 spread rapidly and by 1848 over 4,500 schools catered for 500,000 pupils.

In 1835 Wyse was appointed chairman of a select committee that conducted a detailed investigation into the state of education in Ireland, in particular post-primary education. The report was published in 1838 and severely criticised the existing system of secondary education and the sectarian nature of Trinity College's model of university education.

In the summer of 1839 Wyse was appointed lord of the treasury and Richard Sheil was appointed vice-president of the Board of Trade. They were the first two Catholics since the Reformation to hold ministerial office in a British Government. In 1845 a bill that guaranteed university colleges for Cork, Belfast and Limerick or Galway became law but papal and episcopal disapproval swiftly followed and the colleges were denounced as dangerous to faith and morals.

Wyse was defeated in the 1847 general election, largely due to the opposition of Dr Foran, Bishop of Waterford and Lismore, who campaigned against Wyse and the colleges. However, his talents were recognised by the new government and he was appointed British minister plenipotentiary at Athens, a posting that proved politically challenging. Before departing from London, he was sworn in as member of the British Privy Council and in 1857 he received a knighthood from Queen Victoria. In the nineteenth century no other Irish Catholic reached such exalted heights and was so widely accepted in British ministerial circles. He continued his work in Athens until his death on 15 April 1862.

7

WATERFORD: THE CITY OF CRYSTAL

IN THE BEGINNING

The industry that defined Waterford internationally was revived in the city in 1947 by Charles Bačik, a Czechoslovakian glass manufacturer and the proprietor of four hand-cut glass houses in his native country at the time of the Communist takeover. The post-war political uncertainty inspired Bačik to emigrate and, aware of Waterford's tradition in glass manufacturing, moved to the city with his wife and three children in 1946. Bačik arrived with £300 in his pocket and he raised £5,000 by selling some crates of crystal which he smuggled out of Czechoslovakia. Supported by Dublin jeweller Bernard Fitzpatrick, Waterford Corporation, local investors and his own resources, he began work on a new factory at Ballytruckle in April 1947.

Miroslav Havel, a fellow Czech and a qualified glass engraver who had worked in Bačik's Czechoslovakian factory, became Bačik's first employee in July 1947. Havel, without a word of English, arrived in Waterford on what was intended to be a three-month stay and after a few peripatetic days managed to locate Bačik and his 'glass factory', which at that stage was nothing more than a builder's shed. Havel's luggage included a few books on glass-making techniques and a handful of sample cutting wheels. Havel's planned stay was extended and became a lifetime of service and inspirational input to the Waterford industry. In September 1947, Tom Kennedy was hired as an administrator and became the factory's first Waterford employee. He later became a cutter and a senior foreman.

Havel was initially employed in the construction process and in training local apprentices in the intricacies of glass cutting. The shortage of skilled craftsmen posed a major difficulty for Havel and Bačik at this time and so in January 1948 a glass technology course was introduced at the Central Technical Institute in Waterford. Bačik also travelled extensively on the continent, especially in Germany, in the factory's first year of operation and managed to recruit some skilled craftsmen to work in Waterford.

The factory equipment was initially limited to single engraving and cutting machines imported from Czechoslovakia; a Cork engineering firm manufactured six replica cutting machines. The factory began by importing duty-free Belgian soda glass which was then cut and engraved. Soda glass was manufactured by fusing sand, sodium carbonate and limestone and was mainly used to make bottles, electric light bulbs and window glass. Thin-walled and without lustre, it is at the opposite end of the quality spectrum to the crystal glass for which Waterford became renowned.

Havel spent three months in the National Museum in Dublin, where he carefully studied and created perfect full-scale drawings of each piece of the original Waterford Crystal and other pieces of antique crystal in the museum's collection.

INITIAL DIFFICULTIES

Bačik's initial attempt to expand the business beyond producing cheap soda glass for the domestic market proved difficult. The installation of a glass-melting and blowing facility was an essential prerequisite if he was to fulfil his ambition of establishing a business comparable to what he had developed in Czechoslovakia. A two-pot furnace, designed and built by a French company, was installed; it exploded on its first day of melting, in what has been described as 'a spectacular moment of total technical failure'. It was also a major public-relations embarrassment as Bačik had invited his financial backers to witness what was planned to be the first day of a spectacular future. Bačik was not to be denied and, once again with Fitzpatrick's financial support, a new oil-based smelting furnace manufactured in Edinburgh was installed.

In the 1947–1949 period insurmountable technical and financial difficulties restricted progress and limited the production to beer glasses for the domestic trade. In January 1950 a travelling salesman was added to the staff. Franz Marckwald, a German living in Galway, was the appointee and he hit the road in a second-hand Hillman Hunter on a mission to generate sales for the struggling firm. At this moment in the factory's history Havel visited the Orrefors glass factory near Stockholm to study its production processes. The transition from producing low-value soda glass for the domestic market to producing high-value crystal for the international market was about to take place, but not in the manner that Charles Bačik envisaged.

IRISH GLASS BOTTLE TAKEOVER

In 1950, the Irish Glass Bottle Company (IGB) under the chairmanship of Joe McGrath, 'the richest self-made man in Ireland', took control and Joseph Griffin became the managing director. IGB was the largest supplier of glass jars and milk bottles in Ireland. Bačik was effectively ousted and became a 'director without portfolio', reduced to the role of translator. McGrath's wealth derived largely from promoting the Irish Hospitals' Sweepstake. Government support for the industry through its investment vehicle *Córas Tráchtála* was also forthcoming. Joseph Griffin's accountant son, Noel, was appointed general manager and immediately acted to improve the company's technology. The first customised machines for flat cutting and new diamond-based slicing machines were introduced. It was decided to revive the manufacture of crystal glass and Griffin oversaw the construction of a modern factory at Johnstown, close to the city's gas works (thus guaranteeing a ready supply of furnace gas). This factory, with a blowing section built around a line of ten pots and a cutting section that eventually employed close to 300 craftsmen and apprentices came into production in 1951. For the first time in over 100 years, crystal glass was manufactured in Waterford.

The factory benefited from 'the extraordinary powerhouse of foreign talents in blowing, cutting and stem-making' that Bačik and Havel had assembled but had been prevented from maximising due to financial constraints.

The Johnstown factory was officially opened by Mr Seán Lemass, Minister for Industry and Commerce, on 24 September 1952, and was accompanied by the announcement that, in addition to soda-lime glass, 'production of the highest quality led crystal glass has commenced whether plain, cut or engraved. The company is opening up markets in America, Bermuda, Great Britain, New Zealand and many other countries …' However, a designated design department headed by Miroslav Havel was not established until a decade later; in the first decade of the factory Havel was essentially a director without portfolio, the company's chief designer, but was also available to lend his expertise where and when the occasion demanded. Noel Griffin also travelled to Europe and recruited glass-making talent, particularly stem-makers.

Havel's equivalent in the blowing department was Romanian Joseph Cretzan. A member of a family involved in glass blowing, he entered a glass factory at the age of seven. As a fifteen-year-old, he was conscripted into the German army and returned to glass making in Germany after the war ended. In 1951 Cretzan was appointed to train apprentice blowers in the Waterford factory and at the same time practise his specialist skill on the factory floor. Another German, Kurt Berger, was recruited as a specialist mould maker. He produced the customised wooden moulds used by the blowers to shape the moulten glass.

The new investment made it possible to finance the purchase of the more expensive raw materials required for manufacturing crystal. High-grade, ultra-white silica sand, potash and the expensive red-lead oxide powder were imported and the production of soda glass was abandoned, replaced by the manufacture of crystal glass. As the skill base at Johnstown expanded, stem glasses for port, sherry, wine, cocktails and water, as well as low-stemmed liqueur glasses, round-bottomed whiskey glasses and low and tall champagne glasses were produced along with sets of table glasses and decanters. Diamond-shaped wedge cuts that referenced the original Penrose crystal distinguished these pieces and became Waterford Crystal's most identifiable characteristic.

The blowing department responded to Havel's requirements and produced blown crystal that was relatively thin on the top and became progressively thicker towards the base. This made it possible to insert deeper wedge cuts on the lower parts of a piece whilst leaving the upper area undecorated and was one of Waterford Crystal's characteristic designs.

These suites were marketed using well-known Irish place names such as Lismore, Dunmore, Comeragh, Cashel, Mourne, Royal Tara and Kenmare or women's names such as Alana, Eileen, Sheila, the generic Colleen and Irish Lace in a manner that evoked the 'old country' for the 40 million American residents who claimed an Irish heritage. The Lismore pattern was launched on 23 October 1952 and continues in production to the present day. By 1965, Lismore was the best-selling crystal suite in the USA; four more stem-glass designs were listed in the top-ten sellers. The majority of designs studied by Havel in the National Museum were unsuitable for commercial reproduction. However, the period-piece ranges of the 1950s provided the closest imitation of the late-eighteenth-century Waterford designs and included the turning bowel, sugar and cream bowls, celery vase, claret decanter, claret jug and the Hibernian suite.

WATERFORD CRYSTAL CRACKS THE AMERICAN MARKET

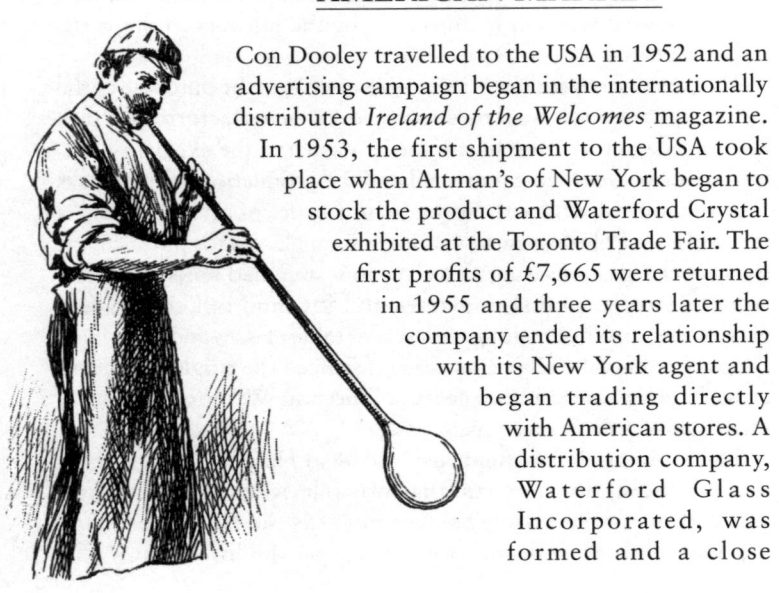

Con Dooley travelled to the USA in 1952 and an advertising campaign began in the internationally distributed *Ireland of the Welcomes* magazine. In 1953, the first shipment to the USA took place when Altman's of New York began to stock the product and Waterford Crystal exhibited at the Toronto Trade Fair. The first profits of £7,665 were returned in 1955 and three years later the company ended its relationship with its New York agent and began trading directly with American stores. A distribution company, Waterford Glass Incorporated, was formed and a close relationship between producer and buyer developed. John Millar, the chief buyer in the crystal-glass department of Altman's New York store, was recruited as president of this company and placed in charge of direct sales and distribution to stores throughout the USA. The 'Collect Waterford' marketing strategy was a Millar initiative and encouraged wealthy Americans to collect multiple Waterford suites. The distribution of the product was tightly controlled and limited to high-end retail stores such as Bloomingdales and Saks in New York, Marshall Field in Chicago and Lord & Taylor in London. It was also sold in some of Dublin's best-known luxury goods stores such as Switzer's and Brown Thomas. The Irish and British markets were relatively insignificant; Waterford Crystal's growth came from its success in America, where the product was a recognised prestige symbol.

COMMISSIONED PIECES

Commissioned pieces of Waterford Crystal contributed to the success of the enterprise from the mid-1950s when the company sold and installed its first chandelier, designed and created by Havel, in Dublin's Ambassador Cinema. Its first significant international commission came in 1965, when members of the Guinness family invited Havel to design sixteen chandeliers for hanging along the central nave of Westminster Abbey in London. Each chandelier comprised of 8,000 separate pieces of crystal with each drop or pendant mouth-blown and hand-cut. The commission was followed by one from the British Parliament to design a suite of drinking glasses with cut stems. In 1967, Jacqueline Kennedy's Waterford vacation included a visit to the glass factory. She did not forget her visit and in 1971 commissioned a chandelier for the President's Lounge in the John Fitzgerald Centre for the Performing Arts in Washington DC. The chandelier was designed by Havel, who also oversaw its installation. The piece which weighed over 500kg, was made up of 4,600 single pieces of crystal and was lit with 115 bulbs. Other notable commissions included the production of a replica of one of the Imperial Russian Romanov chandeliers for the Romanoff Restaurant in Beverly Hills, California, and the chandelier in the lobby of the Shelbourne Hotel in Dublin. Domestic chandeliers were also produced and by the mid-1960s the demand was such that a team of twenty specialists in installation was part of the labour force.

Commissions for speciality pieces provided Miroslav Havel with an additional opportunity to exhibit his talents as a glass cutter, engraver and sculptor. These pieces included a crystal scale model of the Concorde aircraft produced for the French Government in 1974, a paperweight and penholder commissioned by the Bishop of Waterford Michael Russell and presented to Pope Paul VI on the occasion of the canonisation of Blessed Oliver Plunkett in 1976, a paperweight presented to Pope John Paul II by the Polish community in Britain and a scale replica of the Statue of Liberty presented by Taoiseach Garret Fitzgerald to the President of the USA, Ronald Reagan, on St Patrick's Day, on the occasion of the centenary celebrations of the statue in 1986.

Special limited editions were introduced in 1971 and for the first six years were engraved with characters from the Bible that ranged from The Magi to King David. In 1977, Shakespearean characters replaced the Biblical and Romeo and Juliet took their place on Waterford Crystal limited-edition vases.

A successful marketing campaign convinced the promoters of professional sports events to present Waterford Crystal trophies to the winners of major competitions. This practice exposed Waterford Crystal to a different audience and it has been suggested that it was the single most effective marketing ploy. It began with the Bing Crosby Pro-Am Golf Trophy, which at its peak was one of the biggest USA sporting events. Promoters of events outside the USA soon followed suit. The All-England Lawn Tennis Association commissioned a trophy for the centenary of the Wimbledon Ladies' Championship and to celebrate Billie Jean King's record number of Wimbledon victories. Waterford Crystal trophies featured at the French and German Grand Prix Formula One races, the Tennis Master Series and the Volvo Ocean Challenge.

In 1966 Waterford Glass Ltd became a public company. The company was now staffed almost entirely by a local labour force. During the 1960s and 1970s demand for Waterford Crystal expanded dramatically, and began to exceed supply. A new factory at Kilbarry was built which, when completed in July 1973, was the largest manufacturing unit of its type in the world. Its 450,000 square feet occupied a site of almost 10 acres where over 3,400 were employed. A factory was also opened in Dungarvan in 1970 and a lighting factory in Butlerstown in 1979.

Waterford Crystal reached its peak between 1975 and 1985, during which time it cornered up to 30 per cent of the USA crystal market. In 1970, the acquisition of Aynsley China began a series of acquisitions that broadened its commercial base. In the 1980s, computer technology allowed for a more consistent and accurate raw-material mix. The latest furnace design, one that used natural gas instead of oil, was introduced in November 1986, and provided substantial savings. Diamond wheels were introduced into production in 1987 and assisted Waterford craftsmen in creating even more intricate patterns.

DECLINE AND FAIL

However, the glory days were not to last and by the mid-1980s Waterford Crystal was in some difficulty as its share of the USA market began to decline. The purchase of Josiah Wedgwood, the exquisite bone china and earthenware concern, for close to £250 million was seen as a potential solution, partly based on the idea that Wedgwood's status in Japan would create new market opportunities. In 1989, Paddy Galvin became chairman of the company and immediately introduced a series of cost-cutting measures. Waterford Crystal's years of crisis had begun: from 1987 to 1990 the company recorded losses of over £100 million as currency fluctuations added to the company's problems. Pay-freezes, longer working hours, reduced bonuses and over 1,000 redundancies followed. In April 1990, the company's first all-out strike began and lasted for fourteen weeks. An investment of £80 million in 1990 by a consortium led by Sir Anthony O'Reilly that included Morgan Stanley Bank (New York) was critical to the company's survival.

The company began outsourcing some of its products and the Marquis of Waterford range, introduced in 1991, was machine-cut in Slovenia. This was far cheaper to make and sold at a price about 30 per cent below the cost of the traditional lines. It also became one of the best-selling Waterford ranges in the USA. Celebrities were also recruited to promote the brand. Irish fashion designer John Rocha's designs of sets of heavy but clear wine glasses, introduced in late 1997, were an immediate success. Perhaps Waterford Crystal's greatest promotion was the Times Square, New York, New Year's Eve Millennium Ball lowering ceremony in which an estimated 1.2 billion watched as the 6ft diametric crystal ball was lowered down the pole during the celebration of the year 2000 countdown.

Two years later it was a very different New York and sombre ceremony. On 31 December 2001, Mayor Rudolph Giuliani lowered a Waterford Crystal ball, 6ft in diameter and weighing 1,070lbs and composed of 504 crystal triangles engraved with tallies of the presumed dead to memorialize the victims of the 9/11 terrorist attack. On 14 March 2002, a Waterford Crystal American flag was presented to the New York Port Authority Police Department by the President of Ireland, Mary McAleese.

The company's recovery was not to last and in early 2005 the share price fell to a new low. The company's Dungarvan plant was closed and a further 1,800 jobs were lost. Attempts at restructuring failed and in early 2008, 490 job losses were announced, followed by another 280 in October 2008. The end finally came in early 2009. On 5 January 2009, news of the receievership of Waterford Wedgwood Ltd was released and on 30 January it was announced that the Waterford Crystal plant in Kilbarry was to close immediately. Sir Anthony O'Reilly in his statement of thanks to suppliers, customers and staff drew consolation from the 'fact that everything that could have been done, by management and by the board, to preserve the group, was done'. Between 1990 and 2009 O'Reilly and his brother-in-law Peter Goulandris pumped €579 million of their personal resources into the Waterford-Wedgwood company in an effort to save it from collapse; it was a massive losing gamble and a key contributory factor to O'Reilly's bankruptcy in 2015.

In late 2008, O'Reilly unsuccessfully attempted to persuade the Minister for Finance, Brian Lenihan, to provide government security to loans for the firm. The request came at a time when the Irish Government gave a blanket bank guarantee and introduced an emergency budget.

Employees staged an unofficial sit-in designed to prevail upon the receiver, Deloitte, to retain their jobs. The sit-in ended in March 2009.

The pension entitlements of the workforce took a further six years and a legal battle that went all the way to the European Court of Justice to settle. In 2013 the court ruled that it was the obligation of the state to protect pension entitlements in the case of insolvency but it was not until September 2015 that the Irish government finally paid the former employees sums totalling €34 million.

Under the receivership Waterford Crystal and other brands were transferred to a new holding company, WWRD Holdings Ltd. The new owner licensed production of Waterford Crystal products to third-party contract manufacturers in Germany. The sale did not include the factory or visitor centre in Kilbarry. The visitor centre closed its doors on 22 January 2010 and the WWRD group announced that it had signed an agreement with Waterford City Council to open a brand-new Waterford Crystal manufacturing facility and retail outlet on The Mall in Waterford's Viking Triangle. This factory produces crystal pieces using traditional methods and offers guided tours of the plant. Since its opening in June 2010 over 1 million people have taken the guided tour. In August 2016 Gladys Acock from North Carolina became the 1 millionth visitor and was welcomed with a VIP reception.

In 2015 Fiskars Corporation acquired the WWRD group of companies and now operate the House of Waterford Crystal factory, showroom and visitors' centre. This takeover guaranteed the future of Waterford Crystal in its present guise.

8

WATERFORD'S DECADE OF REVOLUTION, 1914–24

WATERFORD AND THE FIRST WORLD WAR

In 1914, John Redmond was the undisputed leader of nationalist Ireland and was poised to achieve a remarkable political victory. He had been the leader of a united Irish Parliamentary Party since 1900 and had apparently succeeded where so many others had failed by delivering Home Rule to Ireland. Redmond was elected MP for Waterford city in 1891 and retained the seat until his death in 1917.

On Tuesday 15 September 1914, the British Prime Minister H.H. Asquith announced that the government would place the Home Rule Bill on the statute book but, influenced by Unionist opposition, opted to suspend its operation for a minimum of twelve months and until the First World War ended. Three days later the bill received the royal assent and its implementation was duly suspended. Redmond's subsequent Woodenbridge speech, calling on Irishmen to join the war effort in a bid to guarantee post-war independence, precipitated a split in the Irish Volunteers as a small minority rejected the policy of cooperation.

The young men of Waterford reacted with remarkable enthusiasm to Redmond's call to arms. An army recruiting office was opened in Parnell Street and 251 recruits were accepted in the first four days of business although recruitment had dropped to less than twenty per week by November 1914. By the end of 1915, an estimated 1,756 Waterford men, approximately 35 per cent of the male population of military age, had enlisted. This figure is even more impressive when it is considered that there was a very high rejection rate on health grounds amongst the city's working-class men who presented for recruitment.

In October 1914, three months after the outbreak of war, Redmond returned to his favourite political stomping ground at Ballybricken and informed his supporters that:

> Home Rule has been carried, and all that now remains is a matter for arrangement ... At the moment in the firing line at the front, Ireland has a larger proportion of her sons than either England, Scotland and Wales and some British forces are being led by Irishmen ... how bravely they are fighting death in the defense of what they believe to be right.

It is estimated that by the end of the war close to 5,000 recruits came from Waterford city and county. John Redmond visited the city again in December 1915 and declared that:

> Waterford has done its duty magnificently. I don't think that there is a city in the United Kingdom which for its population has sent a larger number of its men to the front, and I am certain of this, that there is not a city in the United Kingdom less likely to leave her boys in the lurch.

The war had a positive impact on the economy of the county. The separation allowance increased disposable income and injected cash into the local economy; however, this was offset by a sharp rise in the price of basic commodities such as tea, eggs, sugar, meat, flour, bread and coal. Unemployment in the city and county practically ended as workers were recruited to fill the vacancies created by those who had enlisted. The balance of power between employers and labourers was altered and the latter used the opportunity to secure improved wages and conditions. The Clyde Shipping Company, for instance, granted its workers a war allowance of 5s a week after a short five-day strike early in 1915; agricultural labourers were earning between 1s 6d and 2s a week more in 1915 than they had been a year earlier. The war restricted the ability of foreign-food exporters to access the British market and this created a boom for Irish farmers. Waterford firms also benefited from War

Office contracts. In January 1915, the furniture manufacturing firm of Hearne & Co. won a significant contract to manufacture ammunition boxes. The following month, the Thompson engineering firm moved in to the site of the Neptune Iron Works and began manufacturing shell cases, employing over 200 people. In June 1916, the Waterford South Station, a disused railway terminus, was converted to a munitions plant. Again the firm of Hearn & Co. were the beneficiaries of the remodelling contract and by April 1917 almost 500, mainly female, workers were employed in the manufacture of cartridges.

Unfortunately many of the Waterford volunteers never returned. Tom Burnell, in his book *The Waterford War Dead*, identifies 1,133 Waterford men and 5 women who died in the conflict. Between August 1914 and Easter 1916 over 300 Waterford men died in the ranks of the British Army or the Royal Navy and close to 100 were held as prisoners of war. Three Waterford men were amongst the 1,015 men lost at the Battle of Jutland when the HMS *Indefatigable* was torpedoed by the German battle cruiser *Van Der Tann* on 31 May 1916.

All classes were affected by wartime fatalities with two families in particular suffering dreadful losses. Three sons of James Shine, a retired colonel from Abbeyside, enlisted in Irish regiments and were killed in action. Six sons of Tom and Agnes Collins, who resided in Philip Street in Waterford city, enlisted: Michael, Patrick, Stephen and John were killed in action. Stephen, the youngest, was only sixteen when he was killed in Le Pilly on 19 October 1914 – one of at least thirty-eight Waterford men killed on that day, with another seventy taken prisoner. It was said that after the battle every street in Waterford received a telegram from the War Office carrying the news of a family death. When Christy Collins was badly wounded, the authorities released William on compassionate grounds when they learned of the Collins' family plight. Christy Collins was so badly wounded in Salonika he was presumed dead but returned to Waterford at the end of the war.

The British offensive on the Somme began on 1 July 1916 and fourteen Waterford men died on that day; another thirty-six were dead before the month ended. The 16th (Irish) Division joined the offensive in September and another fifty Waterford men died that month. In 1917, the killing fields for Waterford soldiers were transferred to Passchendaele and between July and September at least seventy more Waterford men died. Those not directly involved in war also tragically lost their lives. In December 1917 two steamships of the Clyde Shipping Company, the *Formby* and the *Coningbeg*, which served the Waterford–Liverpool route, were torpedoed by the German submarine U-62. There were no survivors and sixty-seven of the eighty-three people who died were Waterford natives. The last Waterford casualty in the war was the unfortunate William Hales, a native of Brown Street, Portlaw, who was killed on 10 November 1918, on the eve of the war ending. At the time of his enlistment Hales resided in Detroit in the USA and was a member of the Canadian Infantry.

The contribution of Waterford people to the war effort was commemorated with considerable pomp every Armistice Day for at least a decade after the war ended. The commemorations were organised by the Legion of the Ex-Service Men's Club. The 1922 event was particularly spectacular and was led by the Barrack Street Brass and Reed Band; the Erin's Hope Band, the Thomas Francis Meagher Band and the Legion's Band also took part. The procession ended at Ballybricken, where Captain Willie Redmond addressed the marchers and concluded by expressing the wish that the Legion, 'in each succeeding year, as has been the case in the past ... will find a still greater manifestation of devotion and reverence of our comrades of the days gone by'. In 1923, the Flanders poppy was on sale and 'worn by many' according to newspaper reports and the citywide parade ended with four buglers playing the 'Last Post'. In 1924, an estimated 11,000 paraded in the city on Armistice Day but later in the decade numbers involved fell and the scale of newspaper coverage declined.

Ireland's commemoration of its war dead has always been compromised; at the war's end the country was on the verge of a revolution and those who returned from the war came back to a very different country. In recent times attitudes have changed and the history of Irish First World War volunteers has finally received proper acknowledgement and historical analysis. In October 2013, the Waterford War Memorial Monument was formally unveiled near King John's Castle at Dungarvan. Local man Jim Shine, whose three half-brothers James, Hugh and John died in the war, was one of those who unveiled the memorial. The names of 1,100 Waterford men and women are inscribed in gold lettering on the 50ft-long black granite monument. In Waterford city, the John Condon Memorial was unveiled on Sunday 18 May 2014. The work stands in Cathedral Square, in the city's Viking Triangle. Although named in honour of John Condon, the 'youngest' recorded Allied soldier killed in the war, it is dedicated to 'the men, women and children of Waterford who lost their lives as a result of armed conflict at home and abroad'.

The memorial simply records that John Condon was:

> Known as the Boy Soldier his gravestone in Poelkapelle Cemetery Belgium records his age as 14 when he was killed and his [grave] is one of the most visited Allied war graves in Europe. The Commonwealth War Graves Commission archives record that John Condon was the youngest known battle casualty of the war.

Condon was killed in action on 24 May 1915, during the series of engagements that became known as the Second Battle of Ypres. There is, however, compelling evidence to suggest that the story of John Condon 'The Boy Soldier' is just an enduring myth. The available evidence from official records points indisputably to the fact that John Condon was over eighteen years of age when he died at Ypres. According to his birth certificate, he was born on 16 October 1896 and this is consistent with the ages recorded for John Condon in the 1901 and 1911 Census of Ireland, which means he was eighteen years and eight months old when he died.

Regardless of John Condon's age, his grave stands as an enduring symbol of the futility of war and its devastating impact on young men.

1916 RISING AND WATERFORD

The Easter Rising in Dublin had no immediate impact on Waterford. The county, like most of Ireland, saw no rising in 1916. Seán Matthews assembled a group of his Irish Republican Brotherhood colleagues who marched to the GPO in Waterford but found it occupied by RIC and British troops. Outnumbered and poorly equipped, the group withdrew and in the process any possibility of armed conflict in Waterford was ended. In Dungarvan, P.C. O'Mahony mobilised twelve men to ambush an army ammunition train scheduled to pass through the town. It failed to appear and, after an overnight watch, O'Mahony dismissed his men.

At least fifteen men from Waterford were involved in the Rising in Dublin. Liam Ó Raogáin and Seán Ó Griobhtháin from An Rinn worked as shop assistants in Dónal Ó Buachalla's hardware store in Maynooth. On Easter Monday, together with twelve others, they left Maynooth and marched to Dublin where they slept overnight in Glasnevin Cemetery before reporting to the GPO the following morning. They were directed to Parliament Street and from the roof of the Royal Exchange Hotel they engaged in an exchange of fire with the British military before making their escape. Ó Raogáin returned to the GPO and remained there until the rebels evacuated the building. After surrendering he was detained in Richmond Barracks and on 30 April was one of the first group of prisoners interned in Knutsford. Ó Griobhtháin's involvement ended in Parliament Street and after returning to Maynooth he was arrested, court martialled and sentenced to two years' imprisonment with hard labour which was later commuted to six months.

Liam Raftis served in Boland's Mills under the command of Éamon de Valera and in the confusion of the surrender managed to avoid arrest, although he was suspended without pay indefinitely by the Great Southern and Western Railway for his unexplained absence from work! Thomas Walsh from Tallow, who served under Edward Daly, was the only Waterford man sentenced to death for his involvement but this was later commuted to ten years' imprisonment. Michael Murphy from Cappoquin and Patrick Walsh from Waterford city were also involved as was Richard Mulcahy who was born in Manor Street in Waterford city. Mulcahy was second-in-command in the Fingal Battalion of the Irish Volunteers in north County Dublin, a unit that carried out a number of successful raids that culminated in the Battle of Ashbourne, one of the few successful battles of Easter Week.

At least eight Waterford men were involved in restoring law and order. A reserve battalion of the Royal Irish Regiment based in Richmond Barracks was the first British Army unit involved in the Rising and had six Waterford soldiers in its ranks, two of whom, Lt William Dobbyn and Private Christopher McGrath, later died during the world war. Dobbyn was in charge of the pacifist Francis

Sheehy-Skeffington and the journalists Thomas Dickson and Patrick MacIntryre, the innocent civilians who were shot by Captain John Bowen-Colthurst. He handed the three over to Bowen-Colthurst prior to their murder and told the commission of enquiry into their deaths that he 'was not in a position to say to his superior officer that what he was doing was right or wrong'. RIC member John McGrath, a native of Modeligo, was badly wounded by a sniper at College Street Barracks and was later invalided from the force.

In Waterford, as in other areas, nationalist public opinion was strongly opposed to the Easter Rising. Waterford County Council, like other similar bodies, passed motions condemning the Rising and 'the German dupes' involved. However, signs of change were quickly evident: in May 1916 Lismore District Council passed motions of sympathy to the relatives and friends of the executed leaders and John Redmond was heckled when he visited his constituency in October 1916. Support for the Irish Parliamentary Party began to decline, reflected in the numerical growth of Sinn Féin in Waterford from one branch with 60 members to twelve with 703 members during 1917 although the growth was mainly in the rural part, with progress much slower in the city. The death of John Redmond on 6 March 1918 was followed sixteen days later by a by-election contested by his son Capt. William Redmond. He was a serving officer with the Irish Guards and resigned as an MP for the East Tyrone constituency so he could stand for the Irish Parliamentary Party in Waterford, where he campaigned wearing his military uniform. The Waterford electorate remained loyal to Redmond, and Éamon de Valera, while canvassing in the city, was surrounded by a mob of Redmondite supporters and had to be rescued by his Volunteer minders, but not before he was covered in mud and had his clothes torn. Polling day was marred by continuous rioting and when the votes were counted Redmond enjoyed a comfortable victory over the Sinn Féin candidate, Dr Vincent White (1,242 votes to 764).

The victory was repeated before the year was over. On 25 November 1918, British Prime Minister Lloyd George dissolved parliament and called the first general election in nine years with polling day set for 14 December. The electorate was more than doubled as universal suffrage was introduced for men over twenty-one years of age, and women over thirty who were either householders or married to householders were enfranchised for the first time. Waterford's electoral boundaries were also changed as the number of constituencies was reduced from three to two. Waterford City was combined with its immediate hinterland to form a separate constituency from the rest of Waterford County, where the Sinn Féin candidate Cathal Brugha secured a landslide victory.

Waterford city was different. Dr Vincent White launched his election campaign on 17 November when Rosamond Jacob called on the women of the city to support Sinn Féin as the party that offered women the opportunity to fully participate in public life. The soldiers' wives, 'the separation women', however, were having none of this and, with other Redmond supporters, attacked White at the rally. Irish Volunteer reinforcements were drafted from Cork, Kerry and Clare as frequent outbursts of violence characterised the election campaign. On polling day violent clashes took place outside the polling booths and only police intervention prevented a riot in Francis Street. The Waterford electors kept the faith and Willie Redmond retained the seat but the margin was reduced to just 494 votes. The constituency was one of only two where a Sinn Féin candidate was defeated by an Irish Parliamentary Party candidate, prompting Redmond to designate Waterford as 'an oasis in the political desert of Ireland'.

THE WAR OF INDEPENDENCE (1919–21)

The intensity of the War of Independence varied sharply within the county. In the western half of the county, the West Waterford Brigade of the Irish Republican Army (IRA) engaged in activity from January 1920. This brigade of about 1,800 volunteers was led by Pax Whelan and had four battalions centred on Dungarvan, Kilrossanty, Old Parish-Ardmore and Lismore. The East Waterford Brigade was smaller and a less-effective fighting force. It was led by Seán Matthews and had battalions based in Waterford city, Dunhill-Ballyduff and Gaultier. Arms and ammunition were in short supply and in January 1920 a nationwide campaign against police barracks was authorised. The first attack launched in Waterford on the Ardmore RIC Barracks ended in failure but the attack highlighted the vulnerability of the small rural barracks and accelerated the withdrawal of the police from their rural outposts. The fourth anniversary of the Easter Rising was celebrated by the burning of nine unoccupied barracks across the county as well as the income-tax offices at Lismore and Dungarvan. Confronted by increased violence, RIC members also began to resign; the British Government responded by reinforcing the RIC with army personnel. Across the state, violence escalated sharply in the early months of 1920 and this pattern was replicated in Waterford. A number of policemen were killed, beginning with Sergeant Martin Morgan who was part of a regular weekly pay-patrol that cycled between Kilmacthomas and Lemybrien and was ambushed in September 1920.

The same month the West Waterford Brigade's flying column or active service unit was formed under the command of George Lennon. These were mobile full-time active service units who acted independently or supported battalion or brigade actions as required. The flying column's first major ambush was carefully planned and executed successfully and had its origins in the failed raids on the Ardmore RIC Barracks. On each occasion, military reinforcements were called in from Youghal. In October 1920 another attack began, involving about 100 Volunteers who blocked roads, acted as scouts and kept the barracks and coastguard station under fire. The normal response pattern was repeated and military reinforcements travelled from Youghal. The party of eighteen soldiers and two policemen were ambushed at Piltown Cross on the main Dungarvan–Youghal road. The driver, Private Anthony Leigh, was shot dead and the commanding officer wounded before the party surrendered. Twenty rifles and several thousand rounds of ammunition were captured and the flying column was transformed into a well-armed unit.

The East Waterford Brigade was less active. An attack on Kill RIC Barracks failed in its objectives in September 1920 and an ambush at Kilmeaden in December was called-off when it was realised that the convoy included IRA prisoners. The brigade planned a Piltown Cross-type ambush that involved a force of about sixty men, including members of the West Waterford flying column. An attack was planned on Tramore Barracks in an attempt to lure a relieving military force into an ambush at Pickardstown Cross, which was covered by the IRA from four positions. The plans went wrong and in its first major operation the brigade suffered two fatalities when Michael McGrath and Thomas O'Brien were killed and Michael Wyley and Nicholas Whittle were seriously wounded. The latter was eventually smuggled to England for recuperation. After this, according to Pat McCarthy, 'the East Waterford Brigade practically disintegrated in a welter of blame and recrimination'; several blamed commanding officer Paddy Paul for the debacle.

Martial law was extended to Waterford in January 1921 and this permitted military personnel to try a range of offences by court-martial and introduce a curfew which restricted movement by car and bicycle. IRA suspects were interned. The IRA strategy of blocking roads, digging trenches and constructing barricades forced the military to use predictable routes and made them more vulnerable to ambush. Such tactics were used to organise an ambush at the Burgery, just outside Dungarvan, in March 1921. This was initially successful; a military patrol was disrupted and prisoners and some arms taken. Disastrously the IRA later returned to the ambush scene and an unplanned engagement took place with fatalities on both sides, including the Kilrossanty men, Pat Keating and John Fitzgerald. The body of Fitzgerald was taken into Dungarvan by the military and left in the square on exhibition. Military reprisals followed some days later and a number of houses in the vicinity were occupied and burned to the ground. Bands of soldiers and police also roamed the streets of Dungarvan, breaking windows and doors and removing furniture to burn. In July 1921, the greatest loss of life associated with a single incident in the county took place and was a direct result of the more ruthless tactics adopted by the military. A trenched road in Kilgobinet was filled, following a request from local people to facilitate a funeral. It was subsequently booby-trapped by the military and when it was reopened the mine exploded and killed John Quinn and five of his helpers.

The War of Independence evolved in phases; attacks on police barracks forced the RIC to retreat from the countryside and this phase was followed by the targeting and assassination of individual policemen. At the beginning of the war the county was policed by 240 RIC officers, based in thirty barracks; when the truce was announced on 9 July 1921 the strength of the RIC stood at 270 who were concentrated in twelve barracks. Between 1919 and the truce of July 1921 there were thirty-one fatalities of the war in Waterford; twenty-four of these occurred in the West Waterford Brigade's sphere of influence and consisted of eight members of the RIC, one soldier, five members of the IRA and ten civilians. Two members of the RIC, four IRA members and a civilian were killed in the East Waterford Brigade's district.

CIVIL WAR 1922–1923

Talks between representatives of Dáil Éireann and the British Government concluded with the signing of the Anglo-Irish Treaty on 6 December 1921. Deeply divided opinions on the merits of the Treaty precipitated a vicious Civil War that began on 28 June 1922 and continued until 24 May 1923, when a republican ceasefire was announced. After the ratification of the Treaty by Dáil Éireann, the British Army withdrew and the RIC was disbanded. The military barracks at Waterford and Dungarvan were occupied by the IRA; the Waterford Brigade was officially anti-Treaty but a sizeable minority of its members were pro-Treaty and these occupied the Artillery Barracks in the city. Conflict in Waterford city was short-lived as the city was captured by the Irish Free State army in July 1922; Dungarvan fell in August. For another eight months the county experienced a low-level guerrilla warfare.

The Siege of Waterford
After the initial battles in Dublin between the Irish Free State army and anti-Treaty forces, the anti-Treaty forces, under the leadership of Liam Lynch, placed their hopes on establishing a Munster Republic as a means of frustrating the establishment of the Irish Free State. The establishment of garrisons in Waterford and Limerick and the other towns between the two cities formed a central plank of this policy. The Waterford garrison, commanded by Pax Whelan, was drawn mainly from the Waterford Brigade of the IRA and numbered less than 300 volunteers armed with rifles, revolvers and a few Thompson sub-machine guns. The lessons of the War of Independence were ignored and a static defensive policy was adopted as important public buildings in Waterford, including the Adelphi Hotel, the County Club, the *Munster Express* offices, the post office, Reginald's Tower, the Granville Hotel and Breen's Hotel, were occupied by some 200 anti-Treaty IRA troops. Mount Misery, which overlooked the city, was left undefended in the belief that any troops there were vulnerable and could be easily isolated. The city jail and the Infantry and Artillery Barracks were occupied as second lines of defence. Upriver the bridges at Carrick-on-Suir and Fiddown were blown up and the drawbridges of the railway bridge and the Redmond Bridge in the city were raised and their

controlling devices dismantled. Mobile patrols monitored the city's roads as the republicans awaited the inevitable attack.

The Siege of Waterford is referenced as the key event of the Civil War in Waterford, but to describe the events that took place as a siege is to be generous. The attack on the city by Irish Free State troops proved to be far easier than anticipated. The advance from Kilkenny began on 14 July 1922 under the leadership of Commander-General John T. Prout and his second-in-command Paddy Paul, the former leader of the East Waterford Brigade of the IRA and the man who organised the ill-fated Pickardstown Cross ambush. Any local-knowledge advantage that the anti-Treaty IRA might have had was thus neutralised. The Irish Free State forces occupied Mount Misery and used their single 18lb field gun to subject the republicans to artillery fire. The troops arrived in the city on 18 July and occupied the railway line, roads and the North Quays, and an exchange of fire that lasted several hours took place. The following day the jail and both barracks came under artillery fire. The barracks were abandoned and set alight by the republican forces who withdrew to the jail. On 20 July, 100 soldiers of the Irish Free State army crossed the River Suir 3 miles downriver from the city with the aid of a few small rowing boats and moved stealthily along the river bank. Within a few hours they were on the outskirts of the city. Shortly after midnight soldiers entered the County Club and the Adelphi Hotel through the back door and the two republican garrisons were captured without the exchange of a single shot. The Imperial Hotel and Reginald's Tower were unoccupied and with the minimum of military fuss the main buildings of The Mall were brought under government control.

At the post office, an exchange of fire halted the army advance. The stalemate was broken when the army moved the single field gun from Mount Misery to the North Quay, directly opposite the post office. Six shells were fired across the Suir, destroying the building's interior. The republicans withdrew further down the Quay and briefly occupied the Granville Hotel. The state troops approached the building from the front and rear and forced the surrender of an eighteen-strong republican garrison. Other buildings along the Quay were abandoned and the final outpost of republican resistance centred on the city jail, which was manned by about twenty rebels. After small-arms fire failed to dislodge the occupants, the field gun was again introduced and shelling began. After a few successful strikes on the gate lodge the republicans were forced to abandon the building and escaped the city. The drawbridge of Redmond Bridge was lowered later in the day. The siege of Waterford was effectively over: 'Even by the standards of the Civil War', historian Michael Hopkinson explained, 'the fall of Waterford demonstrated an extreme unwillingness on the part of the Republicans to fight, and a complete failure of co-operation between Anti-Treaty forces'.

There were three military casualties and six civilian deaths. After the capture of Carrick-on-Suir and Clonmel, attention focused on Dungarvan, which after the fall of Cork on 10 August was one of the last towns controlled by the republicans. The advancing army met with no resistance in the county; republican forces, dispirited and disorganised, retreated to Dungarvan. Aware of the hopelessness of the situation, Pax Whelan formed his men into three active service units, retreated to the mountains and began a guerrilla campaign. The effectiveness of this campaign was limited by a lack of public support, and the advantage of local knowledge was gone as the republicans were at war with former comrades who knew the safe houses and the mountainside shelters.

Meanwhile, on 22 August, an Irish Free State army column entered Dungarvan, where they were warmly welcomed. All Waterford towns were now in the hands of government forces.

The Guerrilla Campaign in Waterford

Despite the disadvantages, during the period September to December 1922, the Waterford IRA's active service unit initiated and sustained an intense countywide guerrilla campaign, characterised by sniping attacks on the urban garrison posts and on military patrols and traffic. During this time twenty-five deaths were recorded in Waterford: eleven of the casualties were civilians, four were anti-Treaty IRA and ten were members of the national army. Attacks on railway stations and trains also formed part of the campaign. The Waterford–Dungarvan line was a favourite target of attack. Republicans also initiated a programme of Big House burning and twenty-four houses in the county were destroyed between February and April 1923.

The government responded in September 1922 with the draconian Public Safety Act that established military courts with the power to impose the death penalty for offences that included possession of arms. Michael Fitzgerald and Paddy O'Brien, two natives of Youghal who were captured in Clashmore, were executed in the Waterford Infantry Barracks on 25 January using the powers of this act. Faced with the continuing executions the republican campaign collapsed in the months that followed. In Waterford the county was more intensely patrolled and fortifications were strengthened. In the final act of the war an aggressive sweep of the Comeragh and Knockmealdown Mountains was conducted by the national army. Escape routes were sealed and on 10 April 1923 Liam Lynch, the leader of the IRA, was killed in an ambush in the Knockmealdown Mountains. Other republican losses followed: Austin Stack was arrested in Ballinamult, County Waterford, followed by Todd Andrews. On 11 April, Thomas Keating, the leading Waterford republican, died following an ambush in Coolnasmear. Keating's death stilled the resistance of the Waterford Brigade. On 6 May 1923, the arrest of nine republicans near Waterford city effectively ended the Civil War in the county.

POST-CIVIL WAR WATERFORD

The ending of the war did not bring peace to Waterford as labour unrest and strikes rocked the county; in 1923 there were thirteen strikes that involved more than 3,000 workers, with the gas workers' strike in the city and the farm labourers' strike in east Waterford distinguished by their length and bitterness. During the gas workers' strike the premises was occupied, a soviet was declared and the red flag hoisted before the strikers were evicted by the army. The strike continued for seven months before the workers returned on management terms. The east Waterford farm labourers strike was equally long, violent and bitter and began in May when the workers refused to work a six-day week for a wage of 30s, a reduction of 8s, with all bonuses abolished. Ultimately the labourers were starved into submission and ended the strike on 8 December 1923. Individuals were reemployed as and when the farmer required and on pay and conditions decided by the farmer; the more radical workers were left unemployed.

9

ENTERTAINMENT

Waterford's tradition in entertainment is long and distinguished. Waterford-born practitioners from several disciplines ranging from opera to comedy and from magic to drama and acting have become international success stories.

KEITH BARRY (b. 1976)

Keith Barry, born in Waterford in 1976 and educated in Mount Sion CBS, had a childhood fascination with magic that eventually led to international stardom as a magician, illusionist, hypnotist and mentalist. He first attracted attention when he worked in The Kitchen nightclub in Dublin, where he performed magic tricks for the clients. His initial Irish tour was a success and followed by television shows on RTÉ (*Close Encounters with Keith Barry*), MTV (*Brainwashed*) and *Keith Barry Extraordinary* for CBS in the USA in 2006.

Since his initial breakthrough Keith Barry has starred in over forty international TV shows, his most recent being the prime-time ITV1 show *You're Back in the Room*. His live shows *The Asylum* (2010-11), *Keith Barry-8 Deadly Sins* (2011-12) and *The Dark Side* (2013) have been sell-out successes wherever they played across the world. Most recently he made a brief appearance in the movie *Now You See Me 2*, as well as coaching Woody Harrelson and Dave Franco in the magician's arts for their roles in the Hollywood blockbuster.

Barry has received a number of prestigious international awards including the Las Vegas Review Journal's Mentalist of the Year (2009) and Best Magician in Las Vegas (2009).

VAL DOONICAN (1927–2015)

Val Doonican was born on 3 February 1927, at the family residence of 10 Passage Road, Waterford, the youngest in the family of eight children born to John and Agnes Doonican. After the untimely death of his father from cancer Doonican ended his education at De La Salle College and became an employee of Graves, the builder's supplier and construction company.

The first steps on a journey to the top of the bill at the London Palladium began when Doonican and his friend Mickey Brennan performed around the fire at Boy Scout camps. The duo made their first concert appearance at the Fisherman's Hall in Dunmore East in 1946 and travelled to New Ross for their first paid performance later that year, receiving 10*s* for their effort. Doonican's friendship with Bruce Clarke, another music-mad young man who played steel guitar and piano, led to Doonican's first professional engagement in Courtown Harbour in Wexford in the summers of 1947 and 1948 as a member of a quartet led by Clarke himself.

Bruce Clarke and Doonican later formed a duo and performed on the miniature bandstand on the seafront in Bray, County Wicklow. Niall Boden, who presented a twice-weekly sponsored programme on Radio Éireann, was impressed by the show and invited the duo to add a bass player to their line-up and join him on his show to sing the jingles. The Bruce Clarke Trio became the Donnelly Music Makers and sang the praises of Donnelly's ham, sausages and black puddings twice weekly on Radio Éireann. This provided a significant career boost to both Clarke and Doonican and within a year they were regulars on radio, in theatres and in dance bands, both as a duo and as individuals. Towards the end of 1951 both were members of the resident band at the Olympic Ballroom in Dublin.

Val Doonican emigrated to London in 1951 and joined an Irish-music group, the Four Ramblers, who performed regularly in the BBC radio show *Riders of the Range*. A new career performing in variety shows on music-hall and theatre stages the length and breadth of Britain began, followed by tours of American Army and Air Force bases in Germany.

In 1959, the Four Ramblers toured with the British film star and recording artist Anthony Newley. At a birthday party for Newley, Val Doonican sat on a stool, played the Spanish guitar and introduced, explained and sang an Irish folk song. Newley was impressed and advised Doonican that he had a future as a solo singer. After making his debut as a television entertainer with the musical interlude in *Beauty Box*, a women's beauty and fashion magazine show, Doonican auditioned for BBC Radio by singing 'Delaney's Donkey' and 'Scarlet Ribbon' and was given a temporary spot while *Woman's Hour* was on its summer recess. And then, as he explains in *My Story, My Life*, 'I did something that took the nerve of Old Nick and, even now, I feel a slight twinge of embarrassment when I think about it. I wrote to the man who, at the time was Head of Light Music at the BBC asking if I could have an interview' and to his 'great surprise and pleasure the interview was granted'. He explained that he was in search of work and his preference was for a series of radio shows. His timing was perfect as the BBC were planning a series of light-music shows. Doonican was offered a place on *Dreamy Afternoons*. Explaining the songs he sang became part of Doonican's trademark. The show returned as *Your Date with Val* and was to change Doonican's life. His duties included singing, writing and introducing the show, reading requests and introducing occasional guests.

The radio profile provided a new opportunity and Doonican returned to his old stomping ground of the cabaret circuit but this time as a solo performer, with a schedule that often involved working two different clubs nightly. In 1964, he hosted *Singalong Saturday*, a new BBC TV show, followed by a six-week guest spot on *Barn Dance*. However, it was two guest appearances on the *Sunday Night at the London Palladium* TV show that year that proved a turning point. In Doonican's own words, 'all hell broke loose' and he received several offers to front his own TV show, recording contracts, and opportunities to front summer season shows at leading theatres. Weeks were spent performing in high-order cabaret venues and Doonican topped the bill at the London Palladium.

Doonican's vocal repertoire was eclectic and included folk, novelty songs, and popular easy-listening numbers, which gave him a range of options for his first record. 'Walk Tall' was eventually chosen to launch his recording career with the country number 'Only the Heartaches' on the B-side. Doonican paid for the cost of making the recordings and presented the finished article to whichever record company offered the best deal and the original tape remained his personal property. As a result, he retained ownership of the several hundred songs he recorded. 'Walk Tall' earned Doonican an appearance on *Top of the Pops* and his first album, *The Lucky 13 Shades*, topped the album charts. He followed 'Walk Tall' with four other chart hits and the wonderfully titled *Val Doonican Rocks, But Gently* topped the album charts in 1967. His career was now transformed: long summer seasons in some of Britain's leading resorts such as Blackpool and Great Yarmouth replaced the short-term residencies of the northern clubs, one of the toughest entertainment circuits known to entertainers. In 1970 he topped the bill for a six-month summer-season run in the London Palladium.

Doonican's second series of TV shows was broadcast from BBC's London studio and was given a Thursday night peak-time schedule before transferring to Saturday night. He became famous for his sweaters and the rocking chair in which he invariably sat to sing the final number of his show. In 1966, the shows were attracting a viewing audience of 18.5 million, one-quarter of the total of the British population, and Doonican was honoured as BBC Television Personality of the Year. *Val Doonican Live* successfully returned to its Saturday-night spot in 1976 and continued for twenty-two years.

Val Doonican's career in the entertainment industry was an extraordinary one. He was most successful in the 1965–86 period, when he became a household name in Ireland and Britain. He was, as he claimed in one of his many biographies, 'an overnight sensation after seventeen years'. Doonican maintained close connections with his native city and in 2011 he was made a Freeman of Waterford, having previously acted as grand marshal in the city's St Patrick's Day Parade. He was the first identifiably Irish broadcaster to reach superstar status with the BBC, paving the way for a host of later Irish broadcasters.

THE FLANAGAN BROTHERS

The popular Flanagan Brothers band appeared in dance halls, concert halls and open-air venues across the USA during the 1920s and '30s. Two of the brothers, Louis (b.1896) and Joe (b.1897) were born at 1 Summerhill, Waterford; the eldest brother, Mike, was born in Philadelphia in 1894 before the family returned to Ireland. In 1911, the brothers emigrated to Albany, New York, before moving south to Manhattan's Hell's Kitchen district. The brothers, all self-taught, played at concerts, dances, bars, clubs, and on WNYC radio. Mike (on banjo) and Joe (on accordion) played mainly as a duo but were occasionally joined by Louis on guitar or harp guitar. They performed Irish and Irish-American tunes and songs; at the time American record companies targeted ethnic rather than mainstream markets and the Flanagan Brothers were one of the most successful hybrid bands in New York. They recorded 160 songs for several labels and their discs sold well across the US, Britain and Ireland. The brothers had a keen commercial sense and this heavily influenced their repertoire. Their appeal was to the thousands of Irish emigrants who missed the 'old country' and welcomed anything that reminded them of their heritage. They dressed up in green, white and gold costumes, wrote Irish skits featuring 'Mike and Pat' and sang sentimental Irish-American and humorous vaudeville songs. One of their staples, 'My Irish Molly-O', was a hit in Ireland in the 1980s for Maura O'Connell and De Dannan. They also played and recorded jigs, reels, hornpipes and barn dances such as 'Paddy in London', the 'Rakes of Clonmel' and the 'Cavan Reel'.

ANNA MANAHAN (1924–2009)

There is no real argument as to the identity of the greatest actor to emerge from Waterford. This distinction belongs to Anna Manahan, who was born on 18 October 1924 at Lombard Street, Waterford, and was introduced to acting when a student at the Mercy Convent.

She enrolled in Ria Mooney's Gaiety School of Acting in Dublin in 1944 and this prepared her for entry into professional acting. During the late 1940s and '50s, she worked as a freelance actor in many of Dublin's theatres and served a tough apprenticeship as she toured the length and breadth of Ireland with the fit-up companies.

Anna came to the attention of Hilton Edwards and Mícheál MacLiammóir and was invited to join their Gate Theatre Company. While playing in Limerick, she met Colm O'Kelly, a stage manager, whom she later married. The couple were touring Egypt with the Gate Theatre Group in 1956 when O'Kelly contracted polio and died. Anna went on stage that same night and dedicated her performance in *Dorian Grey* to her late husband. In 1957, she came to national prominence after playing Serafina in the first Irish production of Tennessee Williams' *The Rose Tattoo*. An international breakthrough of sorts came in 1958, when, after a part in the film *She Didn't Say No*, she created the role of Big Rachel in the world premiere of John Arden's *Live Like Pigs* at the Royal Court Theatre in London.

John B. Keane wrote the play *Big Maggie* and its central character, Maggie Polpin, with Anna in mind but unfortunately she was unable to premier the role as she was performing with Tony-nomination distinction on Broadway in Brien Friel's *Lovers*. On her return a special staging of *Big Maggie* was held in Dublin's Gaiety Theatre.

In 1998, Anna travelled to New York with the Druid Theatre and starred in *The Beauty Queen of Leenane*, directed by Garry Hynes, where she earned a Tony Award for Best Performance by a Featured Actress in a Play for her portrayal of the dark and manipulative old woman, Mag Folan. She was recommended for the role by the play's author, Martin McDonagh, who remembered 'the woman who played the housekeeper in the Irish R.M'. She played the Mag Folan role in every performance of McDonagh's play, from its first staging at the Druid Theater in Galway, through its London premiere (1996) to its Tony Award-winning Broadway production of 1998–99. Manahan's last stage role was in the 2005 production of the one-woman monologue *Sisters*, written especially for her by Declan Hassett. It toured Ireland and travelled to Colorado and Broadway.

Anna Manahan enjoyed a successful television career that included roles in RTÉ's first rural-based soap opera *The Riordans* and in Hugh Leonard's *Me Mammy* (1968–71) for the BBC. She took the title role *Leave it to Mrs O'Brien* in the 1980s and played the cook, Mrs Cadogan, in *The Irish R.M.* (1983–85). She returned to soap opera as Ursula in RTÉ's urban serial *Fair City* (2005–09). She also appeared in sixteen films, among them *Hear My Song*, *A Man of No Importance*, *Ulysses* and *The Portrait of the Artist as a Young Man*.

In the words of Alan Stanford, 'She was a force of nature. She was a talent of enormous proportion and density. She was the unique and wholly singular Anna Manahan. She was a child of Waterford – a badge she wore with honour and pride her entire life'. Anna Manahan was awarded the Freedom of the City in 2002 and considered herself 'very lucky to have been born in Waterford'. She returned permanently to the city in 1994, residing with her brothers Joe and Val. This enabled her to work more closely with the Red Kettle Company, the Waterford-based professional company, founded in 1985, that became one of the leading touring theatre companies in Ireland.

GILBERT O'SULLIVAN (b. 1946)

Raymond Edward O'Sullivan was born on 1 December 1946. The family resided in the city's Cork Road before emigrating to the UK in 1953, settling in Swindon a year later. After graduating in 1967 from the Swindon College of Art, O'Sullivan moved to London to further his musical career. Initially contracted to April Music, he sent some demo tapes to Gordon Mills who at the time managed Tom Jones and Engelbert Humperdinck. Mills was impressed and O'Sullivan transferred his recording allegiance to MAM Records where Mills acted as both his manager and producer.

In an era of long hair and colourful clothes, O'Sullivan's image was different: changing his name to Gilbert, he hired a Charlie Chaplin jacket, endured a pudding basin haircut, school tie, a flat cap and long trousers (the short trousers were only used in photographs). Over a four-year period O'Sullivan recorded ten singles, beginning with 'Nothing Rhymed', which reached the Top 10 in Britain, and four Top 5 albums. He was an international star in 1972 and became the biggest selling British-based artist in the world when 'Alone Again (Naturally)' reached No. 3 in the British charts and topped the USA Billboard Hot 100 chart for six weeks, where it sold 2 million copies and earned O'Sullivan his first gold disc. O'Sullivan collected the Ivor Novello Songwriter of the Year award. His first UK No.1 was 'Clair', an anthem to Mills' three-year-old daughter, which ended with Clair's giggles especially recorded for the single.

The movie *College* inspired a new image for O'Sullivan: the cloth cap and short hair were consigned to history and O'Sullivan grew his hair and wore college-style jumpers embroidered with a large letter G. In 1973 'Get Down' topped the UK charts but the follow-up, 'Ooh Baby', only scraped into the Top 20, and after this O'Sullivan only scored one more Top 10 hit in Britain. A bitter split in 1977 with manager Mills, which ended with a High Court appearance, effectively curtailed O'Sullivan's recording career for five years and in the 1982–87 period no new material was released. However, O'Sullivan won the legal battle, being awarded £7 million in damages for an exploitative contract that had deprived him of a just proportion of the income his songs had generated. The case set a legal precedent and several other artists benefited from O'Sullivan's initiative.

Gilbert returned to live performances in the early 1990s and released his twenty-third studio album, *Latin ala G*, on 8 June 2015. Uniquely, he has only ever performed or recorded his own material; there is no place for cover versions in his repertoire.

Gilbert O'Sullivan's relationship with his native city became a little prickly in the 1990s after a less-than-enthusiastic response to his hometown concert at the city's Forum venue. The resentment inspired O'Sullivan to exclude Waterford from future tour lists: 'I would hate to go through what happened in the mid-'90s playing in front of a half-empty theatre which prompted me to say "never again" when it came to Waterford. To go through that again in any of the places I call home would destroy me'.

O'Sullivan is also significant in the music industry as a result of his successes in two landmark court cases. As a young singer the contract he had signed with his manager was exploitative. In 1982, O'Sullivan initiated legal action and was awarded damages as it was judged that he had not received a just proportion of the income his songs had generated. The judge also ordered the return of the singer's master tapes and the restoration of his copyright. The case set a legal precedent and several other artists benefited from O'Sullivan's initiative.

In 1991, Gilbert O'Sullivan returned to the courts, this time in New York where he engaged in the first-ever hip-hop law suit against rapper Biz Markie who had sampled 'Alone Again Naturally' without permission The presiding judge noted that 'the defendants ... would have this court believe that stealing is rampant in the music business and, for that reason, their conduct should be excused'. Gilbert O'Sullivan was awarded 100 per cent of the royalties earned by Markie's 'Alone Again' and the sound of hip hop was radically altered by O'Sullivan's success.

HAL ROACH (1927–2012)

John Roach was born in Waterford in November 1927 and began his career in entertainment after winning a local talent contest as a boy soprano. He initially toured with an illusionist and specialised in magic but later switched to comedy with outstanding success and adopted the name Hal Roach. He spent over sixty years in showbusiness, wrote all of his own material and was particularly popular with American tourists visiting Ireland with an act based on the traditional tourist image of Ireland. His twenty-six uninterrupted years in Jury's Irish Cabaret in Jury's Hotel in Dublin earned him a place in the Guinness Book of Records for the longest-running residency of a comedian at a venue.

The self-styled 'Missionary for Humour' with his catchphrase 'Write it down, it's a good one' placed the emphasis on family-friendly entertainment and was openly hostile to the use of bad language as a means of entertainment. His international profile extended to Australia, New Zealand, the USA, Canada and Great Britain and he shared bills with Frank Sinatra, Jimmy Stewart, Connie Frances, Judy Garland, Ingrid Bergman and all the leading Irish comics from Brendan Grace to Brendan O'Carroll. Roach performed for five USA presidents and was honoured by his appointment as Grand Marshal of the Washington St Patrick's Day Parade (1999). He recorded twelve albums and eight DVDs, wrote ten books and was a regular on the winter months' cruise-ship circuit.

Those attending a Hal Roach show were entertained by jokes like the following one liners:

You know it's summer in Ireland when the rain gets warmer.

You've heard of the Kerryman who was disqualified from the tug-of-war for pushing.

THE ROYAL SHOWBAND

Ireland experienced an entertainment revolution during the early 1960s as the era of the big bands ended and showbands began performing a mixed musical programme, specialising in cover versions of the hit songs of the day. The Clipper Carlton Showband led the revolution, wearing flamboyant suits and introducing impersonations and a comedy routine in their stage programme. Waterford's The Royal Showband secured an unrivalled place at the top of the Irish entertainment pyramid of the time.

Most of the members began their stage careers with the city's Harry Boland Band in the mid-1950s. Michael Coppinger (accordion and saxophone), Jim Conlon (banjo and guitar), Charlie Matthews (drums), pianist Gerry Cullen and Tom Dunphy, a bass-guitar-playing skiffle devotee, were all members of the Boland Band. Brendan Bowyer, who replaced Harry Byrne in the band, served his vocal apprenticeship as a boy soprano in Mount St Alphonsus, the Redemptorist church in Limerick, where his father was organist, and later at the Dominican church in Waterford after the family returned to Waterford in 1949. Trumpeter Eddie Sullivan completed The Royal Showband line-up. The name was inspired by the city's Theatre Royal; the band made their stage debut in September 1957 and continued working as a semi-professional outfit until 1959. T.J. Byrne became the band's manager in 1958 and, on Easter Sunday 1959, they played their first professional date.

In 1960s Ireland the ballroom doors remained closed for the forty days of Lent; Saturday-night dancing was also out of the question and these restrictions provided opportunities for the leading showbands to tour in Britain and the United States. The Royal Showband played the Irish ballrooms in Great Britain in 1959 and in 1960 began playing in the USA in Bill Fuller's chain of ballrooms in New York, Boston and Chicago. In 1961 the band played the Mecca ballroom circuit in Britain and sold out iconic venues such as the Ritz in Manchester and the Hammersmith Palais in London. The Carl Allan Award for 'the most modern dance band attraction' officially recognised their impact in Great Britain in 1961. At the Liverpool Pavilion Theatre on 2 April 1962, The Beatles played support to the Waterford band and the post-dance advice given by Brendan Bowyer to Paul McCartney has become embedded in the folklore of the showband era: he said that the group could do well if they stayed together.

The Royal Showband released their first record ('Come Down the Mountain Katie Daly') in 1962 and made their television debut at Easter 1963 when Teilifís Éireann broadcast *The Royal Showband Show*, a forty-five-minute feature that showcased the band's ability to reproduce the sounds of Cliff Richard, Lonnie Donegan, Nat King Cole and The Platters. Brendan Bowyer displayed his talent as an Elvis Presley impersonator and the programme ended with Bowyer reproducing the moves that led to Elvis Presley being banned from USA television shows as he rocked to his own version of 'Whole Lotta Shakin' Goin' On'.

The Royal Showband's second record, 'Kiss Me Quick', spent fourteen weeks in the charts and remained at No. 1 for seven weeks. In September 1963 another piece of showband history was created when *The One Nighters*, a film shot on location with The Royal Showband, was released. Brendan Bowyer was now an Irish superstar: his next single, 'No More', topped the Irish charts in December 1963 and remained in the top-selling list for ten weeks. 'Bless You' topped the charts in July 1964 and in August 1964 the band became the second showband to release an album when *The One Nighters* was released. The band were now the undisputed royal family of the showband scene with three No. 1 records, an album and a successful film, and were the holders of attendance records in practically every dance hall in the country.

Just when it seemed things could get no better 'The Hucklebuck', the anthem supreme of the showband era, topped the charts in January 1965, remained at No. 1 for seven weeks and electrified the Irish dance-hall scene. 'The Hucklebuck' was the gift that continued to give and also charted in 1976 and 1981. It was part of the band's repertoire for a number of years prior to its release as a B-side of 'I Ran All the Way Home' in December 1964. It would not have been recorded at all had the band not finished its scheduled three-hour session in the Abbey Road studios in London about thirty minutes early and, on the prompting of Walter J. Ridley, one of EMI's top record producers, availed of the time to record another track. The song, written by Andy Gibson, originated as a dance-band instrumental in 1940s New York, and when it was first released (by the Paul Williams Orchestra in 1949) it topped the *Billboard* rhythm and blues charts. Words were later added by lyricist Roy Alfred and it was subsequently recorded by several artists across a range of musical genres. It was immensely popular in the black community in the 1940s and 1950s. Tommy Dorsey, Benny Goodman, Louis Armstrong, Chubby Checker, Frank Sinatra and Quincy Jones have recorded 'The Hucklebuck'.

The band embarked on a new phase in its career in the autumn of 1966 when it completed a four-week residency at the Desert Inn in Las Vegas. They returned to the USA during Lent of 1967 and their sojourn included a residency at the Stardust Hotel on the Las Vegas Strip. The band fine-tuned their repertoire for these performances and four dancing girls were included in the cabaret routine customised for Los Angeles. The final years of the original Royal Showband were spent between the USA and Ireland; the band was Las Vegas based from January to June and returned for the summer Irish ballroom circuit. Absence made the dancers' hearts grow fonder and on their annual return the dance halls were again packed. However, the band began to unravel and attempts to sign Brendan Bowyer and Tom Dunphy as front men for new showbands helped to destabilise the band. The original Royal Showband performed its final show on 29 July 1971 in the Stardust Hotel, Las Vegas.

Jim Conlon retired from the business and a new super-group of leading showband personalities, The Big 8, fronted by Bowyer and Dunphy, was formed. The Royal Showband continued but at the beginning of 1974 only Charlie Matthews and Michael Coppinger remained of the original band. It performed for the last occasion on 9 February 1974 at Bantry, County Cork.

WILLIAM VINCENT WALLACE (1812–1865)

William Wallace was born on 11 March 1812, in Colbeck Street, Waterford city, in the same house as the actor Charles Kean. A piano and violin virtuoso, conductor, and composer, he might well be Waterford's most famous musical export but the city can claim very little credit for his expertise. His father, Spencer, a native of Ballina,

County Mayo, was a member of the 29th Worchester Regiment that were based in the city at the time of William's birth. The elder Wallace was an excellent musician and was responsible for his son's early musical education. The regiment was transferred to Mayo within a year of Wallace's birth but returned in 1825. At this stage William was already a proficient pianist and clarinet player. He received tuition from Otto Hamilton and John Ringwood, the organist of Christ Church Cathedral. The family moved to Dublin in 1826, where William joined the new orchestra of the Theatre Royal. Wallace was appointed organist at Thurles Cathedral in 1830, an appointment that necessitated some teaching duties at the Ursuline Convent to the pupils and young nuns. William fell in love with one of these young novices, Isabella Kelly, converted to Catholicism and took the name of Vincent for his baptismal name. The couple married in 1831. They returned to Dublin where William re-joined the Theatre Royal Orchestra.

Paganini's virtuoso violin performances at the Dublin International Music Festival (1831) proved to be a defining moment in William's career as they inspired him to perfect his own violin playing and to study composition. His first violin concerto was performed in Dublin in 1834.

He emigrated to Australia in 1835 and, after spending some time in Hobart, eventually settled in Sydney, where his performances earned him the title 'The Australian Paganini'. He opened a musical academy and dabbled in sheep farming but these ventures proved to be financially disastrous. Faced with mounting debts, Wallace abandoned his family and clandestinely departed from Australia in February 1838. He travelled to Valparaíso, Chile, where he was welcomed by the city's British community, performing his first concert there in June 1838. His peripatetic existence continued and he travelled to Buenos Aires, Lima and the Caribbean before arriving in Mexico City in 1841, where he conducted a season of Italian opera to critical acclaim. Cosmopolitan New Orleans was his next port of call, where he arrived on New Year's Day 1842 carrying a violin and little else. After captivating the city with solo piano and violin concerts, he moved northwards and performed in Philadelphia and Boston and arrived in New York in 1843. He was again feted as a piano and violin virtuoso and became a member of the original New York Philharmonic Orchestra. Unwise business investments in a furniture-and-piano manufacturing business consumed his musical income and after a series of farewell concerts he departed for a tour of Europe.

In the mid-1840s William settled in London and began to compose operas. *Maritana* proved to be a sensation when it was premiered in the Drury Lane Theatre on 15 November 1845; one leading music critic claimed that the work achieved 'the most complete success ever witnessed within the walls of an English Theatre'. *Maritana* is one of the earliest operas in the Spanish idiom and tells the story of a young gypsy girl who fulfils her dream of becoming a lady at the Royal Court in Madrid. It was also one of the earliest operas to include some of the principal songs of the score in the overture.

His second opera, *Matilda of Hungary*, premiered in Drury Lane in February 1847, again to critical acclaim, but was less successful commercially. William was forced to abandon work on his third opera, *Lurline*, due to failing eyesight. He again became unsettled and travelled extensively as the conductor of a concert party that toured in central and South America and spent some years in New York where he worked as a pianist, conductor and salon composer. He developed a relationship with a young pianist, Hélène Stopel, and the couple had two sons, Clarence and Vincent. They returned to London in 1856 and Wallace completed *Lurline*, which premiered in the Covent Garden in February 1860. He followed this with *The Amber Witch* (1861), *Love's Triumph* (1862) and *The Desert Flower* (1863).

In 1864, William and Hélène moved to Paris to enable the composer to receive treatment for a heart condition; the couple then moved to the south of France, where William died on 12 October 1865. Waterford has not forgotten William Vincent Wallace and on 17 September 1994, a bust of the composer, located at The Mall outside the entrance to the Theatre Royal, was unveiled by the Ambassador of the USA Jean Kennedy Smith. A magnificent new plaza on the edge of the River Suir was officially opened in 2001. Named the William Vincent Wallace Plaza, it is considered to be one of the finest open-air performance areas in Ireland.

10

SPORTING WATERFORD

County Waterford, according to the Census of 2011, has a population of 113,795 but its record of sporting excellence is out of all proportion to its population. Apart from the county's high-profile GAA activities (Waterford is one of the few counties to compete at senior level in hurling, Gaelic football, camogie and ladies' football), the county has several other distinctions in sport: a Waterford athlete has competed at every Olympic Games since 1980; Waterford United FC has won six League of Ireland soccer titles; Ciara Grant was Ireland's most capped women's soccer international with 105 caps when she retired in 2013; Waterford owners, trainers and jockeys have a distinguished record in racing; Waterford Wildcats Basketball Club has won several national titles and Tramore Golf Club has won four Irish Senior Cup titles over the past forty years. The following ten sportspeople have been chosen as a representative sample of the county's sporting magnificence.

CRAIG BREEN

Elite rally-driver Craig Breen was born in Waterford in 1990 and began his racing career in karting, competing in the European circuit. He switched to rallying in 2009 and in his first year in the sport won the Billy Coleman Award for the Young Rally Driver of the Year. In 2010, a victory in the Pirelli Star Driver Shootout enabled Breen to compete in the World Rally Championship (WRC) in the inaugural WRC Academy series in 2011. Breen won the title with an extraordinary final rally in Wales after trailing the overall leader, Egon Kaur, by twenty points. This earned Breen and his co-driver Gareth Roberts a first-prize cheque of £500,000 and promotion to the Super 2000 WRC (S2000) but tragedy struck in a rally in Sicily when the pair crashed and Roberts died as a result of his injuries. Breen returned to racing and victory in the last three rounds of the championship in Wales, France and Spain earned the Waterford driver his second successive world title. Breen's talent was rewarded in 2013 when he secured a work's drive with Peugeot in the European Rally Championship, and in each of his three seasons in the championship he finished in second or third place overall. In April 2015, Breen won the Circuit of Ireland Rally. Driving a Peugeot T16, Breen and his co-driver Scott Martin finished 6.5 seconds ahead of their nearest rival, Kajetan Kajetanowicz. 'I've wanted to win this rally since my childhood hero Frank Meagher won it in 1992', he told reporters after the victory. 'I can't believe it. This means more to me than anything else in the world'.

In 2016 Breen made the breakthrough to world rallying at the elite level when he was contracted to the Citroën Total Abu Dhabi World Rally Team to compete in the WRC, the Formula 1 of rallying, and with it came the opportunity to drive factory-manufactured cars for the first time in his career, racing against the best drivers in the world. Breen was the first driver from the Republic of Ireland to reach this exalted level. He finished in eighth place in his first WRC drive at Rally Sweden and in July earned his first podium place when he finished third in the iconic Rally Finland. At the end of the season, Breen and his co-driver secured a two-year contract with Citroën Racing in the FIA World Rally Championship where Breen will drive the Citroën C3 WRC Concept car.

NIAMH BRIGGS

Abbeyside-native Niamh Briggs was born in 1984 and has been one of Ireland's leading female rugby players for almost a decade. Briggs began playing rugby with Dungarvan RFC in 2005 before moving to Clonmel RFC, a senior club, and then to the UL Bohemians RFC in Limerick. In 2006 she made her interprovincial debut and since then has been involved in seven Munster interprovincial title-winning sides. Briggs was first capped for Ireland in 2008 against

Italy in the Six Nations Championship and was capped for the fiftieth time against Scotland in March 2015. In the 2013 season Ireland won the Six Nations title and completed the Grand Slam for the first time. Briggs was the leading scorer in the campaign, contributing three tries and kicking twenty-eight points. Briggs' contribution to this campaign was recognised when she was selected as the Munster, Ireland and international rugby player of the year.

On Tuesday 4 August 2014 Briggs played a lead role in one of the greatest days in the history of Irish rugby when Ireland defeated New Zealand in their pool game of the World Cup. In the first meeting of the countries in a women's international, Ireland beat the four-times and reigning World Champions 17–14. Briggs' contribution to the win included a superb touchline kick to convert Alison Miller's try and she then held her nerve to kick a difficult penalty to secure the stunning victory. This was the first occasion an Ireland team defeated New Zealand in rugby football, and it was the first defeat of the New Zealand 'Black Ferns' team since 1991. The women's winning run was ended by England (40–7) at the semifinal stage of the World Cup, and they were beaten 25–18 by France in the third-place decider.

In 2015 Briggs succeeded Fiona Coghlan as captain of the Ireland team and captained the country to its second Six Nations title. She made her first appearance for Ireland in Rugby Europe Women's Sevens Grand Prix in Kazan, Russia in June 2016 and also competed in the rugby sevens qualification for the Rio Olympics. In 2016 Niamh Briggs was ranked at number one in a list of the most talented current female sportspeople in Ireland by Joe.ie.

PETER CROTTY

Peter Crotty is the only Waterford boxer to have experienced Olympic competition. Crotty, 'the ironman from Dungarvan', was born in County Waterford in 1925 and engaged in his first boxing contest as an eleven-year-old. After leaving Dungarvan CBS, he worked in construction and as a docker in the local harbour. At the time, Dungarvan was a town without a boxing club so Crotty joined the St Mary's Club in Clonmel. The distance to Clonmel made training there difficult (he was known to occasionally walk the 26 miles from Dungarvan to train and make the return journey on foot also), so most of his workouts took place in the FCA Hall in Dungarvan. Crotty regularly trained in splendid isolation, acting as his own coach, and used an old-army bag stuffed with rags as his punch bag. The 'iron man' reputation was earned for his courage and ability to absorb incredible punishment in the ring.

Crotty won his first Irish welterweight title in 1949 and became the first boxer to win four titles in succession in the weight. Crotty's defeat in the opening round of the 1952 Olympic Games was a particular disappointment for the Irish team as he was expected to contend for a medal. His heavy-body punching secured the opening round against Harry Gunnarsson (Sweden) by the 'proverbial mile' according to the Olympic Council of Ireland's *Official Report*. In the second round, Crotty was head-butted by his opponent and suffered a severe cut to the eye. The referee intervened to speak to Gunnarsson about his use of the head, ordered the fight to continue, but then examined Crotty's wound and stopped the fight. Although not disqualified, Gunnarson took no further part in the competition. Crotty retired from boxing in 1952.

JOHN KEANE

John Keane is regarded as one of the greatest hurlers in the history of the game, a reputation secured by his ability to outplay Mick Mackey, another one of the sport's all-time greats. This standing was given recognition in 1984 when he was selected at centre-back on the GAA's Team of the Century and confirmed in 2000 when he was selected in the same position on the Millennium team. John Keane was born in Waterford in February 1917 and began his hurling career in Mount Sion School. Success came almost immediately; in 1934, while still a minor, he played at full-back on the Waterford hurling team that won the Munster and All-Ireland junior titles. He made his senior championship debut in 1936 and was ever-present on the Waterford team until 1950, except when injury prevented him from lining out in 1944. He captained Waterford on seven of the fourteen seasons in which he played. He was a member of the first Waterford team to win a Munster senior hurling title in 1938 and was also part of the team narrowly beaten by Dublin in the All-Ireland final. A decade later he was still a key figure in Waterford hurling and in 1948 a rejuvenated Keane added power to the Waterford attack from the centre-forward position. The switch paid off spectacularly in the All-Ireland final with Keane scoring 3-2 as Waterford defeated Dublin 6-7 to 4-2 and became the twelfth county to win the All-Ireland title.

Keane's leadership qualities were particularly recognised by the Mount Sion Club; he captained the club from 1939 to 1952 and led them to eight county Senior Hurling Championship titles. John Keane belonged to an era when the Railway Cup Interprovincial Championships were supremely important competitions; he was selected on nine occasions for the Munster team and won seven Railway Cup medals.

Prior to his death John Keane embarked on a remarkable journey during which he visited some of his old hurling rivals including Jim Langton in Kilkenny, Jack Barrett in Kinsale and Jackie Power in Tralee. After visiting Power, Keane was travelling to Limerick to visit his great rival Mick Mackey when he was taken ill and died on the roadside near Tarbert, County Kerry, on 1 October 1975 at just fifty-eight years of age.

SEAN KELLY

Sean Kelly from Curraghduff, County Waterford, was introduced to cycling when he competed in the Carrick-on-Suir cycling street leagues in 1970 organised by the Carrick Wheelers Cycling Club. These races marked the humble beginning of the career of a cyclist who was to top the world rankings for five successive seasons, 1984–1988 inclusive. Kelly decided to turn professional in 1977, a decision hastened by a suspension in 1976 that prevented him from competing in the Olympic Games in Montreal. This was as a result of a clandestine trip to South Africa accompanied by Pat and Kieron McQuaid in October 1975, in defiance of an international ban on athletes competing in the country at the time. The three had ridden in the Rapport Toer, using assumed names as part of a Great Britain team. They were unfortunate in that Richard Burton and Elizabeth Taylor were celebrating their second honeymoon in South

Africa at the time and the event was covered by the British media. A suspicious reporter photographed each member of the team and sent the images back to London for identification.

Kelly first signed professional terms with the Flandria team and won the first of his five Tour de France stages in 1978; following this with two stage wins in the Vuelta a España in 1979. Compared to what was to follow, Kelly's early career as a professional cyclist was unspectacular – he was considered to be a specialist sprinter, in his own words: 'brave, a little bit crazy and fast'.

After a breakthrough in 1982, when he won the Paris–Nice stage race, the green jersey in the Tour de France and a bronze medal in the World Road Race Championship, he was a dominant figure in professional cycling for the rest of the 1980s and into the early 1990s. Apart from his five stage wins in the Tour de France, his portfolio of victories include four separate green jerseys in his fourteen starts in the Tour, victory in the Vuelta a España (1988) along with sixteen stage wins in the race. He recorded twenty-six separate wins in the 1984 season. He has eight victories in the Monument Classics to his credit; the monument classics are Milan–San Remo, the Tour of Flanders, Paris–Roubaix, Liège–Bastogne–Liège and the Tour of Lombardy.

The success of Sean Kelly and Stephen Roche introduced professional cycling to Ireland and the Nissan Classic became a major part of the Irish sporting calendar in the 1980s. Kelly won the inaugural race in 1985 and again in 1986, 1987 and 1991. The 1985 victory included a legendary time-trial performance from Carrick-on-Suir to Clonmel in which he averaged close to 50km an hour for the 21km journey and overtook the Dutch riders Teun Van Vliet (who started one minute ahead of him) and Adri Van der Poel (who began two minutes before him). Stephen Roche, who finished the stage in second place, was forty-nine seconds slower.

Kelly also won the Tour of Switzerland on two occasions (1983, 1990), the Tour of the Basque Country on three occasions (1984, 1986, 1987), the Tour of Catalonia (1984) and the early-season Paris-Nice stage race for an incredible seven successive occasions (1982–88). He won a second World Championship bronze medal in 1989; in the course of his professional career Sean Kelly rode for eight professional teams, Flandria (1977–78), Splendor (1979–81), Sem-France Loire (1982–83), Skil, (1984–85), Kas (1986–88), PDM (1989–1991) and Festina-Lotus (1992).

Sean Kelly was also a mould breaker in professional cycling. He was the first truly great English-speaking rider to compete in professional cycling in Europe.

JOHN LEDINGHAM

John Ledingham from Tinnock, near Clashmore in west Waterford, began horse riding as a six-year-old; he was formally introduced to the sport as a member of the West Waterford Pony Club and won his first RDS Championship at the age of fourteen. His ambition to become an international show jumper was fired when he travelled to Canada and the USA with an Ireland junior international team in 1968. Ledingham joined the Irish Army cadet school in 1976 and progressed to the Army Equitation School at McKee Barracks in December 1977, quickly becoming one of the army's leading show jumpers. He spent twenty-five years at the school, retiring with the rank of commandant.

Ledingham represented Ireland on sixty-three occasions in Nation's Cup competitions, beginning in 1980 and included fifteen appearances in the Aga Khan Trophy at the RDS in Dublin. He is one of the few riders to have jumped on five Aga Khan winning teams (1984, 1987 and 1990 on 'Gabhran' and 1995 and 1997 on 'Kilbaha'). John Ledingham was also a member of winning Nation's Cup teams in Chaudfontaine (1987), La Baule (1994), Aachen (1995), Zagreb (1997) and Athens (1999). He represented Ireland three times in the World Championships, three times in the European Championships and in the Olympic Games of 1988 at Seoul. He was selected to represent Ireland at the Atlanta Games of 1996 but was forced to withdraw when his mount, 'Kilbaha', was taken ill at Stansted Airport on the first leg of his journey to Atlanta.

His first significant victory came in 1981, when he represented the army at the World Military Championships and was part of the Ireland team that won the team title in show jumping and finished second in the three-day event. Riding 'Kilcoltrim', he shared in three successive Puissance victories at the RDS before winning the title in 1989 with a clearance of 7ft 5in.

In 1984, riding 'Gabhran', Ledingham won the Hickstead Derby for the first time after a three-way jump-off with European Champion Paul Schockemohle and Nick Skelton. He won the event again in 1994 and 1995, riding 'Kilbaha'. The 1994 victory was achieved with two brilliant clear rounds and the first prize of £35,000 was augmented with a bonus of £5,000 awarded to the rider going clear twice. He repeated the feat in 1995, again winning after a jump-off and repeating the double-clear round feat for the first time in the event's history. Hickstead was good for Ledingham as he also won three successive Speed Derbies (1993–95) there, riding 'Castlepollard' on each occasion.

Ledingham retired in 2000 and since then has been immersed in the management and coaching of the sport.

JOHN O'SHEA

Thirteen Waterford players have been capped for Ireland in international soccer, but there is no debate as to the identity of the county's greatest soccer player: John O'Shea has represented Ireland on 115 occasions and made close to 400 appearances for Manchester United. O'Shea was born in Waterford in April 1981 and began his career with city clubs Ferrybank and Bohemians. He signed for Manchester United in 1998 and made his debut in October 1999 in a League Cup match against Aston Villa. O'Shea spent most of the next two seasons playing in the club's reserve team and was loaned to Bournemouth and Royal Antwerp in Belgium, before breaking into Manchester United's first team in the 2002–03 season. At the end of the 2011 season he signed for Sunderland and by the end of the 2015–16 season he had made 161 appearances for the struggling Premier League side.

During his United career he won a Champions League medal (2008), five Premier League titles (2003, 2007, 2008, 2009 and 2011), an FA Cup medal (2004), three League Cup titles (2006, 2009 and 2010) and a World Club title (2008).

O'Shea made his debut for the Republic of Ireland on 15 August 2001 as a substitute in a friendly match against Croatia and was capped for the 115th occasion in the 2018 World Cup qualifying match against Serbia. His 100th cap was earned in the UEFA Euro 2016 qualifying game against Germany on 14 October 2014 and he marked the occasion by scoring one of the most important goals in the history of Irish football, a last-minute effort that kept alive Ireland's hopes of qualification for the finals.

O'Shea's versatility was a prize asset for both Manchester United and Ireland and during his career he played in every position in his club's defence, attack and midfield. This included a single appearance in goal against Tottenham Hotspurs in February 2007. Having used all three permitted substitutes, Sir Alex Ferguson looked to John O'Shea to replace Edwin van der Sar after the goalkeeper retired due to an injury seven minutes from time at White Hart Lane.

SEAMUS POWER

The successful West Waterford Golf Club has produced some of the finest golfers to emerge in Ireland since the club's foundation in 1993. The finest of these players has been Seamus Power, a member of a strong GAA family, who was born in April 1987 and joined the West Waterford Club in 1999. He made remarkable progress and won three Irish Youths titles (2005, 2007 and 2008) and was runner-up in 2006, a feat unequalled in the history of Irish golf. He represented Ireland at junior and senior level and won a golf scholarship to East Tennessee State University, where he became the No. 1 player and won a number of important college titles. He also lowered the college's all-time record for a 54-hole tournament when he captured the Jerry Pate National Invitational with a fifteen under-par total for 54 holes.

After graduating, Power turned professional and joined the minor e-Tour circuit (2011-14) where a second-place finish secured him a spot in the qualifying school for the Web.com Tour in 2014. Power obtained a place in the final play-offs in West Palm Beach Florida where he was one of only two players to break par in every round. He finished the six-round challenge on 16 under par, in a tie for fifth place, and secured a first-class card on the Web.com Tour for 2015. On 1 May 2016, Seamus Power became the first Irish golfer to win on this circuit with a 12 under-par single-stroke victory in the United Leasing and Finance Championship in Indiana, which earned him a cheque of $108,000. More importantly, this victory also brought very valuable ranking points that contributed to Power's overall ninth-place position on the tour at the end of August and this earned Power a coveted USA PGA Tour card for 2017. He made his debut on the USA PGA Tour on 16 October 2016 at the Safeway Open played at Napa, California.

The withdrawal of Rory McIlroy, Shane Lowry and Graham McDowell gave Power a place on Team Ireland for the Rio Olympic Games. Power performed superbly and with rounds of 71, 67, 74 and 67 finished tied for fifteenth place overall in the sixty-man field.

TOM QUEALLY

Tom Queally is the most successful Waterford jockey with close to 1,000 victories to his credit in flat racing. Dungarvan-native Queally was born in 1984 and rode his first winner at Clonmel in April 2000. As apprentice to Waterford trainer Pat Flynn, he was crowned Champion Apprentice in 2000 with twenty-eight winners to his credit.

He moved to England, joined the stable of Barney Curley and landed the Champion Apprentice title in the UK in 2004 with fifty-nine winners. Queally's major breakthrough came in 2009 when he saddled five Group 1 winners and became first jockey to trainer Henry Cecil at Warren Place in Newmarket. The Cecil-Queally partnership enjoyed considerable success and included twenty-one Group 1 wins and Queally's first Classic win with 'Frankel' in the 2,000 Guineas. 'Frankel', the wonder horse, once described as a 'lightning strike of genetics, which may not be repeated for 100 years', was introduced to the racing public in 2010 and displayed his special talent with a six-length victory in the Group 1 Dewhurst

Stakes at Newmarket. Queally ended the 2011 season with 100 winners and over £2.56 million in prize money. Queally rode the first of his four successive century of winners in 2008 and achieved his best seasonal total of 109 wins in 2009. Frankel, the 'Usain Bolt of horse racing' according to Queally, was retired unbeaten after fourteen wins at the end of the 2012 season with career earnings just short of £3 million and was officially ranked as the best horse by both *Timeform* and the World Thoroughbred Racehorse Rankings Committee since the latter began its official classification in 1977. In 2014, Tom Queally opted to become a freelance rider.

JOHN TREACY

John Treacy was born on 4 June 1957 in Villierstown, County Waterford, a small village located about 5 miles from Cappoquin. Treacy attended St Anne's Secondary School in Cappoquin and the folklore that he ran home from school each evening is only partly true. In his Leaving Certificate year, he did run home from school each evening but not by the direct route, which only covered 5 miles. At this stage, he was a member of St Nicholas AC in Ring, County Waterford where Fr Michael Enright, Jim Costin and John Harty were formative influences. Treacy achieved success in schools' and junior athletics (he had two third places to his credit in the World Junior Cross Country Championships in 1974 and 1975 and a silver medal at 5,000m in the European Junior Championships). Providence College, Rhode Island, was Treacy's university of choice from the many who sought the Villierstown athlete. Treacy thrived in the USA and was transformed from a very good international-standard junior athlete to a world-class senior athlete. In his last season at Providence College, Treacy captured the imagination of the Irish sporting public with a superb but unexpected victory in the World Cross Country Championships in Glasgow. He defended the title in heroic fashion in 1979, in the highly pressurised atmosphere at Limerick where at least 25,000 attended. The dual victory confirmed his stature at the pinnacle of international distance running.

At the Moscow Olympics, Treacy sensationally collapsed in the final lap of his 10,000 metres heat as he was on the verge of qualifying for the final. He showed remarkable powers of recovery and qualified for the final of the 5,000 metres where he finished seventh, just 1.7 seconds away from a medal place. After a number of injury-restricted performances in the early 1980s Treacy resigned from his Dublin employment and returned to the USA where he became a full-time athlete and prepared for the 1984 Olympic Games. He linked up with cardiologist Dr Dario Herrera, who devised a training programme for him. Scientific analysis pointed Treacy towards the marathon distance and by April 1984 the decision was made to race the event in Los Angeles. Treacy also entered the 10,000 metres but was disappointed with his ninth-place finish in the final. The men's marathon was held on 12 August 1984 and assembled the finest field in the event's history. Treacy raced brilliantly and finished in second place in a new Irish record time of 2:09:56, becoming only the fourth athlete representing Ireland to medal in the Olympic Games in an athletic event. Since then only Sonia O'Sullivan has achieved a similar distinction.

Treacy subsequently raced in a number of big-city marathon races, winning the 1992 Los Angeles Marathon and finishing third in the famous Boston Marathon in 1988, setting a new Irish record of 2:09:15, which remains unequalled to the present day. He ended his serious competitive career with a victory in the Dublin City marathon of 1993 in a time of 2:14:40.

John Treacy was inducted into the Irish athletics Hall of Fame in 2009.

BIBLIOGRAPHY

Books and Articles

An Introduction to the Architectural History of County Waterford (Department of the Environment, Heritage and Local Government, n.d)

Barrow, John, *A Tour Round Ireland* (John Murray, London, 1836)

Blake, Tarquin, *Abandoned Mansions of Ireland: More Portraits of Forgotten Stately Homes* (The Collins Press, 2012)

Burnell, Tom, *The Waterford War Dead: A History of the Casualties of the Great War* (The History Press, 2010)

Cooper, Matt, *The Maximalist: The Rise and Fall of Tony O'Reilly* (Gill and Macmillan, 2015)

Cowman, Des, *The Making and Breaking of a Mining Community: The Copper Coast County Waterford 1825-1875+* (Mining Heritage Trust of Ireland, 2006)

Doonican, Val, *My Story, My Life: The Complete Autobiography* (JR Books, 2009)

Egan, P.M. *History, Guide and Directory of County and City of Waterford* (P.M. Egan, n.d.)

Graham, B.J. and L.J. Proudfoot, *Urban Improvement in Provincial Ireland 1700-1840* (The Group for the Study for Irish Historic Settlement, 1994)

Hall, Mr and Mrs S.C. Hall, *Ireland: Its Scenery, Character and History* (Hall Virtue & Co, n.d.)

Hansard. Joseph, *The History Topography and Antiquities (natural and ecclesiastical), with Biographical Sketches of the Nobility, Gentry and Ancient Families, and Notices of Eminent Men, & c. of the County and City of Waterford Including the Towns, Parishes, Manors and Seats* (Joseph Hansard, 1870)

Havel Brian F., *Maestro of Crystal: The Story of Miroslav Havel and His Role in Waterford Crystal* (Curragh Press, 2005)

Bibliography 143

Hearne, John. M. 'Irish Enterprise, English Alchemy and the Creation of a Brand: The Waterford Glassworks, 1783-1823', in John M. Hearne (ed.), *Glassmaking in Ireland from the Medieval to the Contemporary* (Irish Academic Press, 2010)

Hearne, John M., 'Quaker-enterprise and the Waterford Glassworks, 1783-1851', in *Decies; Journal of the Waterford Archaeological and Historical Society*, no. 54, 1998

Hopkinson, Michael, *Green against Green, The Irish Civil War* (Gill & Macmillan, 2004)

Hunt, Tom, *Portlaw, County Waterford, 1825-1876: Portrait of an Industrial Village and its Cotton Industry* (Irish Academic Press, 2000)

Hunt, Tina and Audrey Whitty, 'The Industrial Design of Waterford Glass, 1947-c.1965', in John M. Hearne (ed.), *Glassmaking in Ireland from the Medieval to the Contemporary* (Irish Academic Press, 2010)

Hutton, Arthur Wollaston (ed.), *Arthur Young's Tour in Ireland (1776-1779)* (George Bell & Sons, 1892)

Irish, Bill, *Shipbuilding in Waterford, 1820-1882: A Historical, Technical and Pictorial Study, 1820-1882* (Wordwell, 2011)

Keogh, Daire, *Edmund Rice 1762-1844* (Four Courts Press, 1996)

Lees-Milne, James, *The Bachelor Duke: A Life of William Spencer Cavendish, 6th Duke of Devonshire, 1790-1858* (John Murray, 1998)

Lewis, Samuel, *A Topographical Dictionary of Ireland, 2 vols* (S. Lewis & Co., 1837)

Long, Colm, *Random Waterford History: A Day by Day Miscellany of Waterford History* (Self-published, 2013)

Montgomery-Massingberd, Hugh and Christopher Simon Sykes, *Great Houses of Ireland* (Laurence King, 1999)

McCarthy, Pat, *Waterford and the 1916 Rising* (Waterford 2016 Commemoration Committee, 2016)

McCarthy, Pat, *The Irish Revolution, 1912-23: Waterford* (Four Courts Press, 2015)

McEneaney, Eamonn, *Discover Waterford* (The O'Brien Press, 2001)

McEneaney, Eamonn with Rosemary Ryan (eds), *Waterford Treasures: A Guide to the Historical and Archaeological Treasures of Waterford City* (Waterford Museum of Treasures, 2004)

McParland, Edward, *James Gandon: Vitruvius Hibernicus* (A. Zwemmer Ltd)

Ó Ceallacháin, Donnchadh, 'The Temperance Movement in Waterford, 1839-1841' in Julian C. Walton (ed.), *Decies; Journal of the Waterford Archaeological and Historical Society*, no. 52, 1996

Ó Cadhla, Stiofán, *The Holy Well Tradition: The Pattern of St. Declan, Ardmore, County Waterford, 1800-2000* (Four Courts Press, 2002).

Perry, Barbara A., *Rose Kennedy: The Life and Times of a Political Matriarch* (W. M. Norton and Company, 2014)

Powers, Jane with Jonathan Hession, *The Irish Garden* (Francis Lincoln Ltd, 2015)

Proudfoot, Lindsay J., *Urban Patronage and Social Authority: The Management of the Duke of Devonshire Towns in Ireland, 1764-1891* (The Catholic University of America Press, 1995)

Prunty, Jacinta, *Margaret Aylward 1810-1889: Lady of Charity, Sister of Faith* (Four Courts Press, 1999)

Russell, Ian and Maurice F. Hurley (eds), James Eogan (executive editor), *Woodstown: A Viking Age Settlement in County Waterford* (Four Courts Press, 2014).

Ryan, Trisha, 'How East Met West: A Typological Explanation for Dromana Gatelodge' in *Decies; Journal of the Waterford Archaeological and Historical Society*, no. 69, 2012

Ryland, R.H., *The History, Topography and Antiquities of the County and City of Waterford, with an Account of the Present State of the Peasantry of that Part of the South of Ireland* (J. Murray, 1824)

Smith, Charles, *The Ancient and Present State of the county and city of Waterford: Containing a Natural, Civil, Ecclesiastical, Historical and Topographical Description Thereof* (W. Wilson, 1774)

Tubridy, Ryan, *JFK in Ireland: Four Days that Changed a President* (Collins, 2010)

Walton, Julian, *On This Day in Waterford*, Vol. 1 (Frank O'Donoghue in association with Julian Walton, 2013)

Walton, Julian, *On This Day in Waterford*, Vol. 2 (Frank O'Donoghue in association with Julian Walton, 2014)

Newspapers

Cork Examiner
Irish Times
Munster Express
Waterford Chronicle
Waterford Mail
Waterford News and Star